SEVEN KEYS TO TEXAS

SEVEN KEYS TO TEXAS

by

T. R. FEHRENBACH

TEXAS WESTERN PRESS

The University of Texas at El Paso
1983

TEXAS WESTERN PRESS
The University of Texas at El Paso

Library of Congress Catalog Card No. 82-074272
ISBN 0-87404-069-8

CONTENTS

By the same author

COMANCHES: *The Destruction of a People* 1974

FIRE AND BLOOD: *A History of Mexico* 1973

THE FIGHT FOR KOREA 1969

THE UNITED NATIONS IN WAR AND PEACE 1968

LONE STAR: *A History of Texas and the Texans* 1968

GREATNESS TO SPARE: *The Heroic Sacrifices of the Men Who Signed the Declaration of Independence* 1968

F. D. R.'S UNDECLARED WAR 1967

CROSSROADS IN KOREA 1966

SWISS BANKS 1966

THIS KIND OF WAR 1963

FOREWORD

There is something special and different about Texas and Texans, just as there is something special about Israel and Jews, or France and Frenchmen.

Texas is only one state (although the largest of the historic forty-eight) of the American Union, but its boundaries enclose more than a mere administrative unit of the United States. It is also a state of heart and mind. This may not be an entirely rational state — but then there is not much rational about being French or Jewish, or having powerful notions of blood and soil. Such things spring from the chemistry of history and culture.

That is what this book is all about: It is not facts and figures about Texas, a travelogue, or an apology for the state and people. Nor is it Texas folklore or Texas brag. A full literature of all those things exists elsewhere. However, very little has been written about the chemistry of history as it has worked in the giant crucible of Texas; many have observed and commented — accurately or with prejudice — but few have attempted to understand or explain the origins and causes of present reality in Texas.

While no one denies that there is such a thing as a Texas mystique, the very notion offends many Americans who in this time and place can accept and even admire almost any form of ethnicity except the Old American wrapped up in a sense of territoriality. But there is a true Texan ethnicity, American to the core, American in its origins, American in its intense patriotism — but in some ways divergent from the American mainstream. And at the same time it can be argued that while Texas is constantly changing under the pressures of American society and government, Texans are also influencing the nation as a whole.

The fact is that some Americans happen to be Texans in much the same way that some Britons are Scots and some Germans are Bavarians. Although Texans have been caught up in the same flaccid commercial cosmopolitanism that pervades America coast to coast, and like the Scots and Bavarians, swallowed up by broader nation-states and cultures, they have retained an essential identity.

Texans, in fact, have occupied something like the position of the Scots within the British Empire: provincials who have provided frontiersmen, entrepreneurs, and adept politicians to the greater society while remaining basically provincial. A Texan who goes to Washington or New York may make his mark on the nation, but he remains a Texan. And like Scots, Texans have been both admired for their qualities and despised as barbarians.

Today, this is important beyond the parochial interests of historians and cultural anthropologists. Texas has always engaged the national – and in some sense the world's – imagination, from the Alamo to the embattled Republic to the Cattle Kingdom, the winning of the West and the raw scent of crude oil at Spindletop. Hollywood has always made Texas a favorite locale and theme. However, today what was once the prospect of an empire has become an empire indeed. Texas is one of a handful of truly "imperial" American states, whose society, economy, people, resources, politics, and sheer wealth, increasingly impinge upon the United States.

Whatever Texas represents, it is too important any longer to be regarded as quaint, provincial, eccentric, or perverse.

Texas is growing at almost three times the average national rate – and in Texas what has been called the American Dream has never died.

Americans tend to be present-minded and problem-oriented, dismissing the past like Henry Ford ("History is bunk") — but those who dismiss history can never quite understand the present reality of Texas and the Texans.

The most important keys to understanding Texans — the majority who inhabit and dominate the state — are historical perspectives. No one would try to understand Israel without some comprehension of the history of the Jews, and it is the same with Texas.

This book, then, is largely devoted to historical perspectives, from which the land and people can be seen. These explain the present — and since history is a continuing process — perhaps some portions of the future.

I hope they will prove useful to outsiders, and for that matter, to Texans, too.

January, 1983 T. R. F.

CHAPTER I

THE PEOPLE

TEXAS is a complex state, sprawling across at least five distinct geographical regions with different economies and lifestyles, and it contains every sort of people and subculture.

Texas is far less homogeneous than its image. One third of all Texans are members of minority groups as these are now defined. In 1980, the state ranked second behind California in its number of Hispanics, second in the concentration of Vietnamese, third in black population, and ninth in American Indians.

Texas is twelve percent black, a percentage that is declining. It is twenty-one percent Hispanic, representing a mostly Mexican twentieth-century immigration that is in no sense assimilated. The proportion of Hispanics has risen rapidly, due both to high birth rates and continuing immigration over the past decade. Black population tends to be concentrated in the southeast or north central regions, primarily in the Houston and Dallas-Ft. Worth metropolitan areas. Mexican-Americans remain along the border and Gulf coast, and more than half live in south-central Texas. In the national pattern, more than eighty percent of all non-whites are in metropolitan areas, with the great majority dwelling in the central cities, whether Houston, Dallas, or San Antonio.

In the white population there are very large elements of Germanic descent and important groups of Czechs and Poles.

However, the reality of Texas is shaped by another factor which makes the state seem far more homogeneous than many others.

A majority of Texans are still descended at least in part from Old American stock that entered the Mexican province, the Republic of Texas, or the State of Texas between 1824 and 1900. This majority, despite divisions by class, occupation, and region, still forms very much a single culture and consciousness, and more important, its ethos is dominant, except for a few enclaves, throughout the state. Cultural and economic domination have continued, in fact, where political power has been lost to other groups, such as the Mexican majority in South Texas.

There are the so-called Anglos. "Anglo" is a word frequently misunderstood outside of the Southwest. It should never be equated with WASP. It is true that most white Texans are Protestant and "Anglo-Saxon" in the sense that this term is used in the United States (meaning an amalgam of Northern European races). But the term Anglo-American, or Anglo-Texan, indicates a full participation in the English-speaking American culture as contrasted with adherence to the still-Spanish-speaking Mexican way of life. By this definition, and it is an important one, ethnic groups as diverse as Irish Catholics, Jews, Lebanese, Norwegian, Chinese, Greek, German, Czech, and Polish Americans in Texas are all Anglos and consider themselves such.

The roots of Modern Texas lie in the British Isles, in an ethos that largely failed in Europe but was successfully transmitted to America, and above all, the American West. But if the racial stock and ethos of Texans came largely from the British Isles, the present Texan consciousness was made primarily in America. Texans are less a people transplanted from various parts of Europe or the world than they are a people made in America out of an historic experience.

For the Texans are a people who made their own history. If they carried their language, religion, and much of their cultural baggage across the Atlantic, they created their own consciousness on the passage through the Appalachians, down the Mississippi, through the forests, and across the plains. And they made their mythos in Texas.

And this is the history and mythology that Texans look back upon, not to some dim memory of the old country. Anglo-Texans, even the newly arrived, do not see themselves as refugees or heirs to some vanished foreign grandeur but as conquerors or the heirs of the conquerors of the American continent — and many of them see that conquest, not 1776 and all that, or the War Between the States, which interrupted it, as the transcendental fact of American history.

In this respect Texan consciousness differs profoundly from that of the present inhabitants of Massachusetts, not one in eight descended from Americans who were sometimes forced to kill Indians or be killed by them. It also differs considerably from that of urban residents in the North or Midwest who came, or whose forebears came, directly from the old country to the neighborhood and who know their ethnic history, if at all, only from story or song, having no blood memory of it.

The majority of true Texans, those who make the reality of modern Texas, may live in modern Dallas condominiums or remote ranch houses near the Rio Grande, but they all stem by blood or tradition from that vast trans-Appalachian trek that resulted in the wresting of North America from the wilderness, the Indians, and the Mexicans.

To doubt that experience is to question the whole meaning of their existence, and outsiders should clearly understand this.

The early Texans descended from clans and families, heavily Scotch Irish, who deserted the panoply of Europe, despising its hierarchies and social organism, who also spurned the tidewaters of eighteenth-century British America with its governments, tithes, and taxes, and who plunged into the wilderness. These folk sought land and opportunity, surely — but they were also consciously fleeing something: a vision of the world in which community or state transcended the individual family and its personal good.

These frontier people poured through the Alleghenies by the thousands while the Revolutionary War was being fought, conscious of that conflict only because of British intrigues among the Indians. They had small interest in the civilized America of the Atlantic slopes with its laws and lawyers; they looked inward instead of outward for their destiny.

They spilled over the eastern mountains, at first in defiance of British mandates, later of the wishes of the American government which followed them. How little they thought of government itself is shown by their willingness to leave American jurisdiction, first behind the mountains, later in Spanish and Mexican Texas.

They saw the Indians and forests as obstacles. If French colonists tried to blend with the forest, and the Spaniards with the Indians, the American frontiersmen pragmatically determined to remove both.

The people who began to enter Texas in the 1820s when the Mexican government offered them land on fabulously favorable terms, whether rich or poor were pioneers born out of pioneer stock, restless, ruthless in their ambitions, and rootless until they found what they were looking for. They were already molded and in many ways brutalized before they came, for the Indian wars were not invented in Texas; they began on the Eastern slopes and were cemented in hatred along the old American frontier between the Appalachians and the plains.

Ninety percent of the Americans who entered Texas in its formative years came out of the Southern states and derived from this older frontier. Half, and more than half of the whites, emigrated from the upper South with its forested hills, hardscrabble small farms, distaste for slaves and slavery, and its lingering frontier traditions. The other half, bringing thousands of black slaves, moved from the plantation economies and "black belts" of the Deep South and Gulf bend. These last were the type Stephen F. Austin and the early empresarios much preferred. They were less unruly and turbulent than the buckskinned uplanders, and they brought capital in the form of slave labor and created a quick patina of civilization.

In Texas each of these streams of Southerners recreated a rougher version of the society from which it came. The planters extended the Cotton Kingdom along the Gulf near the widespread rivers. In those days it was believed that only the dark coastal muck could grow cotton, and that the Texas climate was unfit for white labor. Meanwhile, Alabamians and Tennesseans moved instinctively up the rivers, through the post-oak belt, and toward the Indian frontier. Together these two streams of different, yet essentially homogeneous people created a raw, scattered society of large plantations, small farms, and distant ranches through the immensity of East and Central Texas.

Families from the same area of the South tended to settle in close proximity. Tennesseans sought out Tennesseans; Mississippians founded new settlements and new black enclaves.

The planters — "planter" was a title reserved for the farmer who owned at least twenty slaves, and therefore was able to afford an overseer and remove himself directly from labor — were in every sense entrepreneurs and capitalists. This was capitalism in the Southern, pre-industrial fashion, acquiring land, selling crops to acquire more slaves, with which more land could be cleared and worked. It was dynamic in a sense; it was expansionist and pushed the South westward into Texas. On the other hand, it was socially static and never changed.

The subsistence farmers, the great majority in Central Texas, who erected their dog-run cabins beside stump-strewn corn fields, had neither the money nor the debts nor the increasingly elegant life-style of the planters or the small professional groups which served them. On the surface, the poorer whites and larger cotton growers seemed light years removed in condition, yet both held very similar world views. Both were atomistic, Southern-style puritan Protestants, ferociously self-motivated and self-reliant, prideful and intolerant, hard-working and ambitious. Both had a passion for the land; both ruined it in their own interests (there was always more); both were impatient with government (which inevitably followed them) except as it served their wishes and interests; both held a deep suspicion of social organization beyond the family and the ancient county traditions of the English-speaking peoples. Both were literate, with a literary consciousness strongly influenced by the English Bible. Both were politically aware and active, in their own interests.

Their main forms of political cleavage were not between the rich and the poor — their concept of the state made such things meaningless in politics — but over policy. Coastal planters were always more reluctant to revolt against the rule of Mexico, afterward more eager to bring Texas into the American Union. Planters also were never enthusiastic about Secession later on. Propertied men, they believed in the necessary evil of some government.

Texas frontierfolk, meanwhile, wanted basically one thing from government: the removal of the Indians with whom they were continually in conflict. Otherwise, they wanted no banks or taxes, and to be left alone.

Europeans and Mexicans were both amazed and appalled by the furious energy and rapid growth of this American frontier. What other powers took centuries to accomplish, the Anglo-Americans seemed to do in decades. The British government estimated it would take the United States 1,000 years to push settlement to the Mississippi, but settlers who fought in the Revolution were buried beside its banks. Spaniards and Mexicans, all of whose century-long policies to seed people in the Southwest had failed — in 1824 there were only about 3,000 Spanish-Mexicans in all of Texas — saw themselves outnumbered ten to one within ten years of the decision to permit American immigration.

The Anglo-Texans cut down the forests, plowed the land, built schools, and changed the land forever.

Culture clash and political confrontation were inevitable. Both Mexican liberals and conservatives shared a common fright and common distaste for these new people within the gates, who might, in time, had they been incorporated successfully, have changed the course of Mexican society. But although most Texans of property, amiable toward a Mexican regime that had granted them thousands of free acres and for ten years left them very much alone, opposed confrontation, all Texans were prepared to resist the belated efforts of Mexico to assert its authority, collect customs and taxes, and impose garrisons. And what the Mexican population, vastly more organic, politically passive, (and in its upper classes, more genteelly civilized) accepted as natural or inescapable, drove Texans to the barricades — or more precisely, to the Alamo.

This was a meeting of two peoples in the middle of the continent who, whichever ruled, could not ever really understand or respect each other with any degree of ease.

The Texian Revolution grew from causes very similar to the American war for independence against Great Britain, and the Anglo-American enclave wreaked on Santa Anna and the Supreme Government of Mexico at San Jacinto what its forefathers had wrought against the British Crown at King's Mountain.

This war, against ostensibly insuperable odds, created the Republic of Texas and laid the foundation of the Texas mythos. Marches, massacres, and folly, but also grim determination and cold heroism made Texas free. However uncelebrated outside Texas today, San Jacinto was the decisive turning point that settled the fate of the Southwest and the final cornerstone to North American domination of the continent.

The Mexican War was merely confirmation, as Alexander's campaigns were confirmation of a Greek superiority established at Marathon and Salamis.

The Republic of Texas was an improbable but hardly artificial nation, far more cohesive and facing much fewer difficulties than most of the new nations of the twentieth-century Third World. With increased Anglo-American immigration across the Red and Sabine, it expanded its static culture west and south from its original Brazos-Trinity enclaves. But blood called to blood, and practicality among the planters overwhelmed nationalistic romance among the Texan expansionists such as Mirabeau B. Lamar. Texas accepted membership in the Union, over the figurative dead bodies of Northern Abolitionists, and Texan aggressiveness was incorporated into American Manifest Destiny.

As a state, with another tragic interruption in the Civil War, Texas expanded its culture, with many adaptations to time and place, south to the Rio Grande and westward across the Comanche plains and on to the southern Rockies.

The coonskin cap dominated early Texas lore and legend; later the frontier cowman's sombrero replaced it. But the great landowners who exported crops for cash or credits dominated the economy and manners, although they did not always dominate or even control politics. Together, the Texas frontiersman and the capitalist-entrepreneur in a crucible that worked very much like the eighteenth-century American frontier, tended to absorb all other groups except the black slaves and the residue of Mexicans.

The German, Swiss, Alsatian and other agrarian immigrants who entered Texas in large numbers before 1860, making up seven percent of the population, became Anglo-Texans in all but name (and eventually, even in that) except for a few isolated instances. German-speaking groups became the majority in more than a dozen central counties, but contrary to much myth and latter-day romanticizing, they farmed and lived exactly like their neighboring Tennesseans and Alabamians. Their cattle ran free, unfenced, and their houses were built of the same native limestone in the Southwestern style and fashion. Only church spires rising here and there in Texas towns intruded Old World civilization. On the coastal bend, Germans bought black slaves, and sided emotionally and materially with the Confederacy.

In this nineteenth-century frontier crucible, Yankee steamboaters, Presbyterian merchants from Pennsylvania, Anglican planters from South Carolina and even German-Jewish tradesmen who pioneered mercantilism in the Texas towns, were assimilated into local speech and mores. The potato-famine Irish avoided Texas, and the great waves of late-nineteenth and early-twentieth-century Eastern and Southern European immigration into America went elsewhere – deep agricultural depression in the cotton-raising South offered no attraction. The hordes who fled Reconstruction in the war-torn states merely solidified existing patterns, and new agrarian immigrants, mainly from the Slavic regions of the Austrian Empire, hardly changed them. During the last century more Mexicans departed Texas than entered over the Rio Grande.

From the late nineteenth century, immigration was relatively unimportant until the 1970s. Growth, until the 1970s, came overwhelmingly from native natural increase, and from Old American stock, Texans or Americans whose grandparents were born within the United States.

Thus the society and institutions and manners of Texas came mainly from two cultural influences, the Old South and the old Southern upland frontier, combining the courtliness and castes of one with the fierce independence, combativeness, and crudities of the other.

It was an amalgam set before 1860, not to be altered significantly for more than 100 years.

Texas might have emerged more like some Midwestern states, for there was little real difference between its majority of small corn farmers in the post-oak belt and along the fringes of the Great Plains and the sodbusters of Kansas or Missouri — however they became emotionally separated in the Civil War. But Texas had a planter class, whose Southern cultural influence was profound, lasting beyond the destruction of the class itself.

And Texas, for all its heroic history as a Republic, might have become merely another Southern state — but Texas had, and was, and is an eternal frontier.

CHAPTER II

THE FRONTIER

FEW people today would deny that the "frontier" is alive and well in Texas. Observers of the Texas scene never fail to mention such things as the "frontier ethos," the "frontier style," or the "frontier heritage" of Texans, whether the subject is ranching on the Pecos or wheeler-dealering in Houston. The "frontier" in fact has become a cliché. Yet the term and concept stand for something very real in Texas, something which sets the state apart.

Every part of the United States was of course a frontier at one time. However, the frontier was of very short duration in most places once British America had streamed across the Appalachians. The true frontier years, the period of deadly Indian peril, did not extend past a decade on the "dark and bloody" ground of Kentucky. The middle border was primitive and tough, but what was more remarkable historically was the speed with which civilization advanced. Daniel Boone broke trails to new ground no white man had seen, yet lived long enough to be driven to the Rockies and beyond by lawyers. The sons of Tennessee borderers had to look for new horizons, finding them in Texas.

Kentucky was the key to the conquest of the continent; Texas was the culmination.

Outside the Middle South, no other heavily populated region of the United States beyond the original thirteen colonies ever endured a genuine frontier experience, serving as a border and a buffer between American civilization and a wild country of hostile peoples. The forests were felled and villages organized almost overnight. Nowhere, Hollywood "history" notwithstanding, was there any protracted warfare between Indians and white civilians along a defined frontier after the eighteenth century — until Anglo-Americans reached Texas.

Here Americans had to battle for predominance with a different nation and culture (the Mexicans), face a far more dangerous type of warlike aborigine, and master a land whose geography was strange and alien. Here the war frontier lasted more than a generation, and the ecological frontier has seemed to last forever. Here the frontier lasted long enough to imprint itself thoroughly in the people's consciousness, to fashion song and story, create a literature, affect folkways, and give birth to a culture. The frontiers between Christians and Moors in Spain, between Scots and Saxons are gone but they are hardly forgotten. The frontier in Texas is much closer in time, and its memory and effect still green.

Texas is still populated by large numbers of "pioneer" families whose forebears fled from the advance of Mexican armies, whose great-grandparents lived in constant danger from Indians, and whose parents grew up amid what may be described as frontier conditions. While the pedigree of "old" families in Texas is pale beside those of old New England or Virginia stock, Texans are much closer in time, thinking, and feeling to their ancestors than Easterners. Of the latter, few know, or want to know, that Massachusetts Bay once paid bounties for Indian scalps in colonial shillings and lived in fear and hatred of French Canada.

Texas is not the entire West, nor does it represent the total geographic reality and cultural concept, but it is where the

West began, and it is the American region from which the "West" was transmitted north and westward. It is also where the "West" probably remains strongest in popular feeling. Far more Americans pioneered on the Texas frontier than on any other of the American West's ephemeral borders, and their descendants were less diluted by later immigration. Colorado had its frontier days – but Colorado is overrun by out-of-staters (including many Texans) and has succumbed like any Northern or Eastern state to internal regulation and bureaucracy; it might as well be Wisconsin.

Unlike most of the "frontier," Texas actually experienced a history. The difference can be seen in the "frontier days" celebrations that are held all across the Western states, attempting to recall a period of the local past. They are culturally amorphous and historically inaccurate. Texas towns and cities also put on these fêtes, commercially inspired and having nothing to do with the real past whether "Charro Days" at Brownsville or "Buccaneer Days" at Corpus Christi – but Texas also has a vast number of actual battlefields, and it is sprinkled with monuments extolling explicit events that changed history. Like most peoples – but unlike most Americans – Texans have a consciousness of both winning wars and losing them, of being conquerors and also being humbled on their own soil. In short, history has happened to Texans both as Westerners and Southerners, and they are aware of it.

Many if not most Americans seem to want to forget that this nation was not erected by consent but over the bones of countless Indians, Mexicans, and Confederates. Texans are more aware of the reality, symbolized by the shrine of the Alamo, the markers on the battlegrounds, and the statues raised in dozens of drab towns to the Confederate fallen. San Antonio, for example, is the most fought-over city on the North American continent.

People from other regions are frequently amused, or sometimes irritated, because Texas history is taught in Texas schools and colleges; what they overlook is that Texas, as

Texas, has a history and that its history amounts to one-fourth of the total corpus of United States history.

The Republic was born of blood and iron like all historic nations. It rose from the slaughters at Goliad and the Alamo and San Jacinto and the thousand lesser blood-lettings that allowed it to survive. Texas historians have always seen the nineteenth century, the crucible of Texas, as a three-cornered war for the Texas people. Texans fought Mexicans for independence and dominance and cultural survival. They fought Indians for survival and the land itself. They fought Yankees and the federal apparatus itself for sovereignty and regional definition. These wars are over, but their effect lingers.

In many ways Texans, like most peoples, came to define themselves by their enemies — a source of strength, but also of problems for the future.

The *de facto* independence won at San Jacinto in 1836 in no sense ended the conflict between Texas and Mexico. No Mexican government would acknowledge Texas sovereignty, although no Mexican government had the power to undo it. The boundary question both on the south and to the west was unsettled; there was no clear line of demarcation between Mexican and Texan-held territory. For ten years, hostilities continued.

This warfare was real. Texas formed a navy which harassed Mexican shipping in the Gulf and aided Mexican rebels in Yucatan. Meanwhile, the Texans also organized several harebrained expeditions to invade Mexican territory. Launched with more enthusiasm than realistic planning or military science, these ended in disaster, with their members defeated and captured. Distances and desert destroyed the Santa Fe expedition, while the captives from the Mier expedition were subjected to the Mexican practice of decimation — forced to draw black and white beans from a pot; the ten percent who drew black beans were stood against the wall and shot.

The Mexicans considered Texan invaders as pirates rather than prisoners-of-war.

They retaliated by attempting to stir up Texas Indian tribes against the settlers, though Mexican agents had little success. The Mexicans also launched counter-invasions. These were actually military demonstrations and punitive expeditions rather than serious efforts to reconquer the separated province, though on two occasions in 1842 Mexican armies seized San Antonio. On the last occasion, Mexican soldiers arrested and carried away all the prominent Anglo citizens of the town as hostages. These men were incarcerated in the Mexican fortress of Perote until finally released, due to the diplomatic efforts of the United States.

The annexation of Texas by the United States defined and supposedly secured the border at the Rio Grande. But it also caused the Mexican War. The first battles were fought in the Rio Grande Valley, making this area Texan soil. The Treaty of Guadalupe Hidalgo ceded Texas and the Southwest, made the United States the dominant power — which Mexico never again questioned — but it did not make the Texas-Mexico border a safe or settled region.

The river separated two culturally differentiated peoples whose mutual animosity took long in dying. The huge expanse of the border country was remote from the centers of population on both sides, arid and undeveloped, and it remained a region of suspicion, lawlessness, frequent anarchy, and occasional bloodshed for another century.

Between 1848 and 1917 the borderlands of Texas were subjected to banditry, incursions, and reprisals, by both sides. Mexican bandits and cattle rustlers operated from below the Rio Grande, selling stolen stock to Cuba. Hostile Indians also took refuge south of the border, from whence they could carry out depredations with impunity. For many years Indians and bandits made the region between Laredo and the Gulf almost uninhabitable for Texan ranchers, while in the far-western trans-Pecos area forts and ranches were synonymous.

Meanwhile, the Mexican borderlands were not secure from punitive forays by both Texas Rangers and the U.S. Cavalry, to say nothing of the Comanches and Apaches who habitually struck deep into Mexico out of American territory. In the 1870s this raiding reached a crescendo. Spurred by border complaints, Rangers entered Mexico and killed a prominent local citizen as a "cattle thief" while the Cavalry under Ranald Mackenzie crossed the river and burned a number of Indian villages.

The anarchy was diminished, if not entirely ended, by the Porfirio Díaz regime which came to power in Mexico in 1876 — with notable Texan assistance. The border incursions had created diplomatic incidents, and Díaz, less from friendship than from a keen pragmatism, wanted good relations with the United States. He suppressed the border banditry ruthlessly, and the Mexican army cooperated in widespread campaigns against the hostile Indians, conducting operations involving thousands of troops on both sides of the border in the 1880s.

The end of the Díaz regime and the beginning of the Mexican Revolution in 1910 again placed the Texas borderlands in danger. Between 1910 and 1917 Texas was infested with Mexican revolutionaries of all kinds; in fact, Francisco Madero planned the revolution in San Antonio, and Pancho Villa bought his guns in Texas. When the bloody civil warfare in Mexico spread northward to the border towns, their Texas counterparts were flooded with wounded and refugees, while stray bullets frequently fell on the American side. The citizens of El Paso watched battles for Ciudad Juárez from their rooftops, while U.S. troops and many civilians dug trenches along the Rio Grande for safety.

As all authority broke down in Mexico, raiders on horseback swarmed through the Lower Rio Grande Valley, derailing trains, shooting up small towns, robbing and sometimes even kidnapping individual Texans. Most Texans, but few other Americans, know that by 1917 almost the entire Regular Army and hundreds of thousands of National Guardsmen from as far away as Indiana had been mobilized for Texas border service. General Pershing pursued Pancho Villa (he never caught him) in Mexico, and actual warfare between the two nations was only narrowly avoided.

This anarchy and violence created viciousness. Texans, who had by and large admired Porfirio Díaz because he kept order, reacted strongly to violations of the border, and hostility to Mexicans spilled over to animosity toward Mexican-Americans. Between 1915 and 1917 at least 300 suspected "Mexicans" were killed by vigilante action in Cameron County alone, creating fears and hatreds that linger into the present time.

American troops remained on the border until the 1940s and the establishment of stable government in Mexico.

The present era of economic interdependence and good feeling along the Mexican border is only a generation old, and Texans out of a long and bloody history, remain more conscious than other Americans of the eternal possibility of problems along the Mexican frontier — the only border in the world separating an industrial nation and a painfully emerging Third World society.

The Indian frontier was far more dangerous to Texan settlement than the Mexican, even during the turbulent days of the Republic. Few people settled in the south, below the Nueces, but by 1834 Texan colonists were moving high up on the Brazos, clearing farms in the rolling post-oak country of central Texas, and here — while they had not yet trespassed on Comanche range — they came into the range of Comanche raiders.

Here the Texans faced two new frontiers that were outside of American experience. They entered a land where wood and water ran out, and a borderland disputed by the longest-ranging, most fearsome mounted Indian people on the North American continent. Here the frontier paused, at times even recoiling, for forty years, or across two generations. And here was carried out the bloodiest fighting between the white and red peoples since the seventeenth century.

The Indian wars in Texas were different from those in almost all other parts of the United States. They most closely resembled the struggles between frontierspeople and Indians in the eighteenth century, when whites were few in numbers and unprotected by government. In fact, the years 1861-65, when all troops left the border, uncannily repeated the terrible decade in Kentucky, with whites holed up in stockaded settlements while Comanches rampaged throughout the country.

Americans arrived in Texas with a long history of Indian "troubles" and Indian removal but not of protracted Indian warfare. The usual pattern was one of white encroachment, which meant white farmers pressing upon tribal territories as they moved westward. This usually provoked an Indian "uprising" that caused the slaughter of a few whites and the temporary terrorization of all whites in the territory. But the Army or militia would quickly move in, and almost always the natives would be subdued in a single, sustained campaign. This pattern was general from the Appalachians to the Mississippi, except for the forgotten Americans in Kentucky during the American Revolution.

Most Indian peoples were destroyed by minimal military force. First contacts with Europeans left them demoralized by whiskey and decimated by Old World diseases. In this way the Caddos, once the most numerous and advanced of all Texas Indians, had been virtually exterminated by traffic with the French and Spanish long before the entry of Anglo-Americans. The Karankawas of the coast, the Tonkawas of the interior, and the Lipan Apaches of the south, suffered the same experience.

The other part of the pattern was that in the forested country all the tribes were basically agricultural. They lived from corn and only supplemented their diet by hunting. They were bound to the land by their crops. White soldiers could search out their villages and storehouses, force them to fight fixed battles in which they were vulnerable to superior power or military organization. In this way a host of Indian tribes were driven out of East Texas by one campaign in the 1840s. On the orders of President Lamar, Texas troops burned out the "whole rat's nest," missing only the Alabama-Coushattas quite by accident.

In any case, both across America and in East Texas, armed force removed the Indians before there was much bloody contact with white settlement. Abraham Lincoln, as a young Illinois militiaman, took part in one such sorry affair against the Sauk and Foxes.

The old methods did not work in Texas, however, once the frontier line approached Comancheria.

First, the frontier families on the edge of that vast region known as the Great Plains dwelled in the midst of seemingly limitless space in an area potentially rich but lacking timber and water. Great distances separated their farmsteads and ranches, which made them quite vulnerable. The white population rarely averaged more than one person per square mile. There were few towns, no places to "fort up," and no effective way to raise or sustain a real militia.

Second, the Plains Indians of which the Comanches were a part, were a new kind of warrior. Comanches and Kiowas had never planted a seed, never made a permanent camp. They lived by following the bison herds over a trackless, infinite prairie. They had become horse barbarians, incredibly mobile by any known standard. The Comanches, especially, avoided most contacts with whites, almost never allowing Europeans to live among them. They remained powerful in isolation. Finally, out of experience with the Spanish-Mexican frontier, they had become skilled and deadly long-range raiders of civilized settlements.

These tribes had ripped and shredded the Hispanic frontier long before Americans came to Texas. They had in fact destroyed the Spanish dream of North American empire in Texas and were instrumental in the decision of Spanish authorities to let Americans colonize in Texas, where it was hoped they might become a buffer between Mexicans and Indians.

Finally, only in Texas and for the first time since the eighteenth century was a white farming population placed within the raiding range of powerful, warlike Indians, a situation that continued for four decades before the Army at last destroyed them. On the northern plains, Sioux and other tribes threatened trappers or buffalo hunters, immigrants passing through, or the Army itself when sent among them. The Northern Plains wars were essentially wars between Indians and soldiers.

In Texas, it was a war between farmers and primitive warriors, in which the agrarians were outmatched, with profound effect upon Texas development.

This was a fact badly misunderstood beyond the Indian border, whether in East Texas or in Washington. Many believed that if the whites merely left the Indians in peace, the Comanches would reciprocate. However, Comanches were not Cherokees in feathers — war was a permanent state of mind with them.

From the days of British ministries, governments had tried to create a line of demarcation between white and Indian territories; this continued into Grant's second administration. The peacemakers misjudged the imperatives of the two peoples. Anglo-Texans, like the American nation itself, would never have permitted the interior to remain as a "squalid game preserve" held by "stone-age savages." Meanwhile, the mere entry of white civilization into the country quickly destroyed the land for the traditional usage of the Indians. The efforts at peacemaking merely delayed the inevitable and made the conflict more protracted, and thus more terrible.

This was not a battle between right and wrong, but rather, two rights in mortal conflict. It was the most primordial of human struggles, one for cultural dominance or death on the prairies, as savage as any in the Holy Land, with great wrongs done to the other by each side. The frontier suffered forty years of bloodshed because of the weakness or indecisiveness of civilized government, until finally, in the 1870s, government dropped the fiction of the "freedom" of the Plains tribes and took effective action to remove them.

This could have been done with more dispatch, and thus greater mercy, and carried out with more honor by the representatives of civilization. The end, in any case, was destined to be the same. Canada, with a more authoritarian government in the nineteenth century, prevented mass bloodshed on her own Plains frontier. But the eventual incorporation of the tribes into an all-encompassing civilization destroyed the Indian way of life just as surely.

The first historic raid on a Texas settlement came in the spring of 1836, just at the time that Texas was winning independence on the battlefield. A party of Comanches struck Parker's Fort, a stockaded cluster of cabins on the Navasota River in present Limestone County. Before the men, who had been working in the corn fields, came running back with rifles, the Comanches burst into the compound, killed five men and two women, wounding others and leaving them for dead. They scalped Elder John Parker and cut off his private parts; they raped Granny Parker and pinned her with a Plains lance, and they rode off with two young women and three children as captives.

One of the children was Cynthia Ann Parker, who became the mother of Quanah, the last Comanche war chief.

The Parker raid was a precursor to hundreds of others, the beginning of the Comanche terror on the frontier.

This kind of raiding and war was not directed at whites alone, or out of any special hatred. It was the normal mode of Indian warfare, the same sort they waged against Mexicans and each other. While the object of a raid was usually to steal horses, the "murder raid" was just as common. Enemies of all ages and sexes were slain; women were raped; captives were tortured. Neither babies nor old women were spared; however, women and children of an age to be useful as captives were often carried away. Sometimes the captives were later killed; if they survived they were made slaves or adopted into the tribe, according to the captor's whim. Unless they were adopted, women and children often could be ransomed, however in these cases, when they were returned, most of them were demented, and bore the signs of harsh abuse.

The sad business of seeking out and ransoming Comanche captives continued on the plains until the end of the Indians' domination.

White Texans saw Indian warfare as pure atrocity, and they considered the Comanches no better than animals. Their hatred, understandably but unjustifiably, spilled over to all Indians, the inoffensive as well as the hostile. This grim aspect of the frontier must be understood. In distant Philadelphia, men might speak sentimentally of Indians and talk of brotherhood, but on the Texas frontier, fathers who had buried sons burned alive, wives who had found mutilated husbands, and families who spent frantic years searching for lost loved ones, called all Indians vermin and said the only good one was a dead one. Their contempt for any other view, as the Texas historian Walter Prescott Webb wrote, was colossal.

Between 1836 and 1860, 200 men, women, and children were killed each year by Indians on the Texas border; between 1860 and 1875 at least 100 died or were carried off annually. The trek through central Texas cost seventeen white lives per mile.

Compared to the Texans, the Comanches were never numerous. But a mere handful of warriors could terrorize a whole frontier. The settlements were thinly spread, miles between them in many cases, and Comanche tactics devastating. From inaccessible, hidden camps far out on the plains, a war party would ride into the frontier by night, holing up by day, and pass unseen. Often they avoided the outermost settlements, where men were armed and wary, preferring to strike fifty or even a hundred miles behind the actual frontier. They attacked at dusk or dawn, stealthily, brutally, then mounted and raced away, sometimes not stopping until they had reached the safety of the vast plains.

The worst time for the frontier was summer under the full moon, when grass was high for the Indian ponies, and there was light to ride by night. "Comanche moon" was not a romantic term in Texas – the coming of the full moon meant terror.

The agrarian population along the frontier was more helpless than most modern Americans realize. Americans arrived in central Texas on the edge of the Great Plains (then called the American Desert) poorly equipped to conquer either the land or its inhabitants. American agriculture, military organization, technology, and even American law could not cope in a land where water and wood ran out, and mounted foemen, the "best light cavalry in the world," attacked out of a trackless waste that few white men dared to enter.

The Anglos were not horsemen in the Comanche, or even the Mexican sense. Their horses were heavy, grain-fed animals. They lacked the endurance of the Indian mustangs, bred to the Plains; above all, they could not live entirely off the native grasses. The whites also had far fewer horses than the Indians. An ordinary warrior might possess a dozen or more. This gave the Plains people their incredible mobility. On raids, Comanches carried along large *remudas* or strings of ponies; they could change mounts frequently and thus overtake any fleeing enemy while easily out-distancing all pursuit, even by the lumbering cavalry.

American weapons in the 1830s were also inadequate. Muzzle-loading firearms were cumbersome in the saddle; a Comanche could loose a dozen well-aimed arrows, each with the force to drive a shaft through the body of a full-grown buffalo, while a Texas rifleman could fire a single shot. Comanches in fact were so contemptuous of firearms that they had discarded them about 1800, preferring the bow until the advent of repeating rifles in the 1870s.

Comanches avoided attacking a fortified position. The European ethos that made men stand and die at places like the Alamo was foreign to them. This was not a matter of courage. They excelled in hand-to-hand combat, but the sensible code of Plains fighting required the inflicting of maximum damage on the enemy with as little as possible to one's self. Casualties demoralized Comanches, and being magic-oriented primitives, they were fearful of portents and anything that seemed to suggest bad medicine – that the spirits were against them. While unbeatable man-to-man and vastly more adept at fighting in the wilderness than whites, they lacked the Texans' stubbornness and sustained purpose in making war.

Despite movies and myth, the white frontier never conquered or destroyed the Comanches. The farmers and ranchers were never able to do more than avoid their own destruction from raiding. However, the frontier did adapt and establish the means to defend itself. This adaptability was a salient characteristic of the Texas border, in fact, it was one of its greatest strengths. The Comanches, who were caught in a trap of tribal culture, never changed, while on the other hand, the Texans learned and changed quickly.

Texans soon learned to become true horsemen. This came first and most easily with the young people, the children raised on the frontier where a good horse and the skill to ride could be the difference between living or dying. They developed strains of horseflesh better suited to the country while producing men and boys who could stay in the saddle with a Comanche.

People on the frontier also learned how to survive in Indian country.They fortified their homes and dug sod shanties that resisted burning. They went armed at all times and exhibited constant wariness. Comanches usually scouted their victims beforehand, and they chose the careless and less vigilant – a fact rarely forgotten on the Texas frontier.

Texans quickly adapted their agriculture to stock raising on the edge of Comanche country, and also adopted the northern

Mexican cattle culture as it had evolved along the Rio Grande.

Americans came into Texas as corn growers, cotton planters, and pig farmers. These techniques worked so long as the advance stayed within the confines of East Texas, which geographically is an extension of the Gulf South. In the piney woods and on the rich Gulf coastal muck of the fertile crescent, Texans could continue old ways and continue in their old excellences and Southern cultural traps. But as they came out on the fringes of the plains where rain ran out and trees faded into waving grass or went southward across the burning *brasada* of the borderlands, they had either to halt or change.

The pragmatism and adaptability with which they changed their techniques stands out in sharp contrast with the attitudes of Indians and Mexicans, who were culturally resistant to most changes.

Texans who owned livestock had previously herded them on foot in the time-honored British fashion. But on the frontier, they seized upon the entire Mexican cattle culture, even its jargon, from lariat (*la reata*) to buckaroo (*vaquero*). They took up Mexican longhorn cattle, the open range, the ranch, the brand, the male-bonding of the *vaquero* and the values of the *charro*, or Mexican mounted gentleman: courage, skill with horse and rope, semi-feudal loyalty to owner and brand. They took a way of life and infused it with the cold, hard pragmatism of capitalistic enterprise — for the frontier *was* a business, even in its wildest, most "romantic" Indian-fighting years.

The true Cattle Kingdom in most ways was as ephemeral as the true frontier. It was gone when Texas turned from open range into the land of big pastures in the 1880s. But meanwhile, Texas and Texans exploded it north and west across the remaining continent: to Kansas, Colorado, and Wyoming, to Montana and distant Calgary, and from the Pecos to the California mountains. And meanwhile, there was time enough for Texans to stamp forever the image of the Cattle Kingdom into the American consciousness, just as the frontier had impressed itself on them.

The most important, and certainly most celebrated, adaptation of the frontier, however, was a new form of frontier defense. The Republic was too impoverished to establish a regular force to protect the settlements. Even the United States, when it assumed responsibility for the border, lacked a cavalry arm, although foot troops were next to useless in the vast distances of Texas. The first U.S. cavalry regiment was raised for Texas service in the 1850s, but then and later – while these troops eventually scoured the Indians from the Plains – government was too niggardly to provide an adequate constabulary. The Texan frontier's response to this lamentable state of affairs was the Texas Rangers.

The "ranging companies" sprang up almost naturally out of the frontier community. The men were young, unpaid, and un-uniformed, passing casually in and out of service. The captains emerged from the ranks, from a process of natural selection. The frontierfolk fed the Rangers, and the Republic and State sanctioned them.

Many efforts have been made to compare the Rangers to other armed forces and irregular constabularies, from Cossacks to Moss troopers. None is adequate; the Rangers were *sui generis*, entirely a creation of the Texas frontier. Throughout a century they changed many times, but they were never highly organized or disciplined, and they only became a truly professional elite police force in the 1930s, when their role was reduced to that of an investigatory agency. They were an improbable band to win worldwide fame and recognition.

The Rangers are a key to Texas and the society it forged. They were adventurous and courageous – if a man lacked these qualities he had no business on the frontier – but they were also pragmatic and far from foolhardy. (Fools died too easily in Indian country.) Their leadership, which ranged from the classically educated to the unlettered, was remarkable by any standard. Ranger captains were direct, brutal, coldly realistic, no-nonsense men, yet clearly on the side of advancing civilization.

The Rangers adapted themselves to their enemies and calculatedly went them one better. They "fought fire with fire," as they put it, although a historian has written that they were armed with the products of civilized workshops while sloughing off the values of civilization.

Ranger captains understood that the best way to protect the frontier was not to patrol it but to carry war to the Indians — a policy that took a generation for the Army, restrained by higher authority in the East, to recognize. The Comanches were vulnerable to this. They had lived so long in perfect sanctuary on the plains that their camp security was lax, and as a result, Tonkawa or Apache scouts — blood enemies of the Comanches — could lead the Rangers to them. When they could, Rangers fell on Indian encampments exactly the same way Comanche raiders attacked farms and ranches, by surprise, and with swift and bloody violence. They understood Indians, the frontier, and its imperatives.

When Colonel John Moore rode up the Colorado "half way to Santa Fe" and surprised a Comanche gathering in the fall of 1840, he broke the power of the Southern Comanches and ended what had been a wholesale slaughter along the southwestern Texas borders. With the loss of one dead Ranger, Moore shot down more than 100 Comanches. His report states: "The bodies of men, women, and children were to be seen on every hand wounded, dying, and dead."

Whatever history said of these "punitive expeditions" they proved effective. They saved the southern Texas frontier in the 1840s — how much so is revealed by the fact that during the Civil War when all troops left the border, the white frontier recoiled 200 miles eastward in the face of a then much weaker Comanche threat.

Rangers immediately saw the value of Samuel Colt's revolver when no one else in the world, including the U.S. Army, would buy it. It was the answer to the Comanche bow in mounted combat. Jack Hays and his troop, armed with the new six-shooters, became the first Texans to charge and defeat a superior force of mounted Indians. Hays, who with fourteen men destroyed seventy Indians, gave all credit to the six-gun, although he was a tactician of the first order.

The thousand revolvers used by Rangers in the Mexican War made this weapon known all over the United States. Thus Texas Rangers saved Colt from bankruptcy, but they also emblazoned what had become their symbol, the six-shooter, into the American consciousness, where few will deny it still remains.

Superb tacticians, shrewd field psychologists, Rangers calculated the fears of their enemies and worked upon these. In retrospect, the Rangers have seemed wantonly brutal and deliberately bullying and domineering. But the Rangers faced an impossible task in trying to police this frontier. They were almost always heavily outnumbered (creating the legend of the one-Ranger army) by enemies from whom they could expect no mercy or quarter, whether Mexicans, Indians, or badmen. Only by establishing both a sense of inferiority and a real sense of fear in their foes could Rangers prevail.

Thus, Ranger captains successfully played upon the Comanche's dread of "bad medicine." They won several mass mêlées by demoralizing the Indians beforehand by such practices as sniping down a prancing warchief. They cowed Mexicans by exhibiting a cold, passionless ferocity that was psychologically emasculating; a remarkably bitter memory of this exists among those of Mexican race on both sides of the border. In dealing with outlaws or "crazy-drunk" cowboys, they shot first and asked questions later. In the 1870s, when the attention of Rangers turned more to scouring the state of its immense, post-Civil War and Reconstruction population of road agents, bank robbers, and cattle thieves, the fearsome tendency of the Rangers to force confrontations and shoot instead of bringing back prisoners "so that the courts could free them" actually drove some thousands of real and suspected bad characters out of Texas.

The Rangers never halted all the lawlessness and violence, of course, and the Army, not they, waged the final campaigns against the Indians, just as the Army provided the real protection on the southern border. But Texans applauded their efforts, compared their methods to those of other agencies, and despised the latter. For Rangers, born of the frontier, embodied many of the bedrock values of the frontier. They were brutal to enemies, loyal to friends, courteous to women, kind to old ladies; they never gave up, claiming that no power on earth could stop the man in the right who kept "a-coming." These were male values, warrior values. But whatever work they made of the niceties of law and procedure and "civilized" war, there was never any mention of Rangers having oppressed their own people on the frontier – something rarely recorded of similar armed guardians in world history.

There were only a few Rangers, but they created, in truth and in legend, a giant image for Anglo-Texans that no matter how many could or could not live up to it, none could quite ignore.

The true frontier closed by 1881. In that year the last settler was killed by Texas Indians, the last free band of Apaches having been tracked and shot down in their camp in the Diablo Mountains by Texas Rangers. Two years later the rails reached El Paso, spanning the continent from coast to coast. In 1876 there was no permanent white settlement north of Big Spring; five years afterward the whole Panhandle was enclosed by cattle ranches. Windmills and barbed wire – the latter seen by many of the old, open-range generation as the Devil's invention – turned Texas from a country of wild range to a land of big pastures, which it has remained.

However, the "frontier" died grudgingly. The Mexican-Indian warfare, the cataclysm of the War Between the States, the wild country itself, spawned a vast residue of violence across the west and south of Texas. Almost every piece of ground, every water hole, every family on the land, had its private record of confrontations, crime, gunshots, and blood under the sun. No one thinks of Texas as a society of duelists in the nineteenth century, yet here the "duel," with its own frontier codes, killed more men than all the encounters along the Mississippi. Most of the violence was too commonplace to get in the history books. In fact, it was so common that huge chunks of this history have been moved, in fiction, to other locales, simply because the public grew tired of hearing about Texas.

Not for another fifty years after the closing of the frontier in the 1880s would men put off the habit of wearing pistols, and even after that, many if not most Texans kept firearms close to hand.

The frontier experience gave Texans an identity, a feeling of folkhood beyond the reach of Ohioans or Oregonians. The frontier people did not so much "settle" Texas as conquer it. The true Texans — those descended in some way from the nineteenth-century people-making process — understand this even if most cannot articulate it.

Texas was never a refuge for the lowly or oppressed, no matter how many of the lowly sought their fortunes there. It was a harsh land, a frontier where only the strong, the wary, and the competent were likely to survive and succeed. This fact permeated Texan attitudes, attitudes that are still common in the smaller communities of inner America where people are not so much competitive as contemptuous of incompetence. Texans did not condone, and the realities of the land did not suffer the man who carelessly exposed his family in Indian country, or who could not erect a homestead or bring in his cattle or crops. The resources of the developing land were thin; while Texans were cooperative in times of danger or misfortune, every family head was expected to manage for himself. The American frontier was made up of countless, widely separated individual units; it was atomistic, and the idea of social organism was unknown.

These deeply imbedded cultural characteristics still affect Texas society in everything from civic cooperation to labor organization and attitudes toward public welfare. If Texas is still a place where "rugged individualism" is admired, it is also a last refuge for the jackleg. The good citizen is the man or woman who can cope but never burdens or bothers neighbors — a feeling that is not so much merciless but a rejection of the very notion of social organism such as practiced in more hierarchical societies.

Out of the frontier experience, certainly, came much of the Texan's characteristic empirical, hard, non-ideological, and belligerent mentality.

If only a small part of Texas' population ever actually suffered on the frontier, the consciousness of the struggle penetrated and conditioned the whole people, especially those who went beyond the Deep South confines of the pine woods. Frontier problems dominated the Republic's politics; they made and unmade governors of the State. All Texans in some way were caught up in the battle for the land.

There was and still is a conscious belief that Texans chose this country, fought for it, held it, and succeeded where others, Indians and Spaniards and Mexicans, failed. And there is little sympathy in Texas for the opinion that the contest was unequal or that victory was inevitable. The record of sufferings borne on the frontier furnishes dramatic proof to the contrary.

When a Texan talks of his Indian-fighting ancestry, or about how his grandmother survived the wilderness, this is something very different from the casual, if prideful, mention that his daddy was in World War II. The frontier experience was a real struggle for blood and soil and is much more deeply graven into Texas consciousness than anything else that has happened since — however earthshaking in its national or international implications.

CHAPTER III

THE LAND

TEXANS had to battle Mexicans and Indians for their land, but they also had to battle the land itself – a struggle which goes on and continues to shape Texans as much as they have shaped the land.

It is difficult for Easterners or Europeans who have not traversed Texas to grasp the brooding immensity of this land. The state of Texas encloses 265,780 square miles, an area which is larger than the states of North Carolina, South Carolina, Georgia, Alabama, and Florida combined and which far exceeds the total area of France. South Texas alone is bigger than England and Wales together in geographic extent. Distances have always been vast in Texas, and they still are vast, even in the air and auto age. In world terms, however, the population has always been sparse, even though the present population of more than 14,000,000 exceeds that of many nations. The Texas towns and cities are still dots in an immense space. The land dominates, in an almost Russian sense.

Texas spans at least five distinct geographic regions, ranging from the pine-wooded Gulf south to the treeless Gulf coastal plain to a Rocky Mountain ecology in the far Big Bend basin. However, most of Texas beyond the pine woods is a country of rolling hills, broad prairies, rising limestone plateaus, and almost treeless plains, a land of vast horizons, a land where the natural tendency of man and animals is to be volatile and free.

It is a beautiful land, although as in Australia, the first generation of settlers could not appreciate its true beauty — for Texas is also a harsh and curiously fragile land, punishing man and beast with brazen sun and periodic storm, hail and heat, floods and raging blizzards, bugs and bad water. Although Texas lies far south in latitude and its southern tip is dotted with palms and flowering hibiscus, it is part of a continental land mass strongly affected by a mid-continental climate. While warm, humid breezes blow up from the southeastern Gulf, artic winds also howl down from the roof of the world in Canada, roaring across plains that throw up nothing to deter them. The land in most areas is subject to extremes and violent climatic fluctuations, heat and cold, burning summers and ice storms, drouth and deluges.

But the dominant feature of Texas is water, or rather, its scarcity. Half of Texas is well-watered, but from east to west the rain falls increasingly less. The huge tableland beyond the 98th meridian is semi-arid or arid; although only a small portion of the state, in the south, can be classified as true desert, more than half of Texas suffers from a lack of water. Rainfall is uneven. Although the annual rains across most of central Texas equal those of London in total measure, the moisture tends to fall at scattered periods, long dry spells broken by heavy rains, rainy seasons interspersed by months of extreme aridity. The western rivers run too alkaline to be useful.

The reality, and historic tragedy, of Texas is that climatic conditions will not support unirrigated agriculture, known in Texas as dry farming. The soil is relatively good — although Texas is no Iowa — and during wet cycles the country blooms deceptively. In the years of adequate rainfall, most kinds of agriculture could and can be carried out successfully. But the cruel quality of the land is that wet is followed by dry along a vast borderland — a country not so obviously arid that people avoided it, but treacherously holding out a promise to the uninitiated, then blasting their dreams and labors with dust and destruction. Only in the understanding of this ecology can so much of the history of Texas, and the acquired toughness of its people, be fully understood.

Just as the Anglo-Americans who came to Texas encountered a different and more dangerous kind of Indian, they entered a strange and difficult country once they passed beyond the timbers. They attacked this land as stubbornly as they resisted the Comanches — but the land was not as easily conquered as mere human enemies.

Determined to master the land and make it bloom according to the dictates of American civilization, thousands ruined themselves, and the more successful actually ruined much of the land itself. The overgrazing of cattle and the plowing up of ancient, thin topsoils turned to dust thousands of square miles where once millions of bison roamed. It made cactus and mesquite-choked scrub of areas where millions of longhorn cattle, running free, once thrived and increased. The agrarian conquest of Texas destroyed much of it, in a battle that man sometimes won, sometimes lost — in a war in which the outcome is still uncertain.

Texans did none of this damage intentionally, however willfully they proceeded with it. They were ignorant of the land and its imperatives; they tried to fit it to themselves rather than fit themselves to it. The Anglo could not do otherwise: he was trapped as surely as the Comanches in the imperatives of his culture, which demanded that the land be put to use, that land and water be demarcated into private holdings, and the use be for private profit.

As men moved determinedly across the Texas prairies, extension of civilization marked a new struggle for cultural domination, both between new proprietors and man and the land itself.

Indians, and even Mexicans, had put the land to a minimal usage that the Texans instinctively despised. Now the free-range cowmen, who had adapted to the country, left their dead at disputed wire fences and water holes and were subdued by writs and railroads even as they spread the Mexican-derived cattle culture to the Canadian border. But the hordes of hoemen, small farmers who moved recklessly through central Texas, were themselves beaten by nature and disinherited by relentless market forces beyond any Texan's control.

Drouth and falling commodity prices, banks and lawyers, poverty and foreclosure broke more Texan hearts and filled more graves on the prairies than all the wars.

But there were survivors, and the survivors out of the total experience came to see the land, *their* land, as more than mere acreage or a prosaic business. It had been hallowed by their dreams and their sweat and their buried dead. Even the losers, who in their thousands sank into bankruptcy and tenantry and who finally, in the twentieth century moved to city and town, with their children and children's children would remember the struggle and be affected by it.

From this came certain stubborn Texan traits, as strong in the largest cities as in the smallest dusty towns: a hard-driving pragmatic business sense, a desperate belief in growth and "progress" and population increase, and an impatience with most ideologies that did not serve man's mastery over the land.

The land, and the symbolism of the land, and the way it shaped the people is another key to the modern Texan heart and mind.

The entire existence of Texas, past and present, can in some way be described as a land rush, characterized by cycles of land boom and bust. Land, after all, was the reason most Anglos came to Texas, and land, its produce and what can be extracted from it, has remained the basis of the Texas economy.

The advertisements of Stephen F. Austin and other empresarios who brought colonists to Texas in the 1820s also created a vision of empire which was to be lasting. The smell of "empire" lured men to Texas, and something of that scent has lingered to the present day.

The Spanish-Mexican authorities granted land to settlers on terms far more attractive than any that could be procured in the United States. Whereas public lands in the States sold, bad times and good, for hard cash, Mexico made grants of thousands of acres to any who could qualify. They hoped, of course, to create a contented colony as a buffer against both the Indians and future encroachments of the United States into an empty Texas, and the lure was land. But the Mexican government gave away more than land to farmers and stockmen: It gave them freedom from tithes and taxes such as were inflicted upon other Mexican citizens, cessation of custom duties, and during a crucial, formative era, freedom from government itself. So it was that the various Texas colonies became self-ruling, so far as they had any rule at all.

Between 1824 and 1835, Texas became the frontier paradise of America. Thousands of Americans, both poor and substantial, shed their citizenship to acquire Texas holdings. This showed not only the lure of empire in Texas, but also how little the American frontierfolk was conscious of its own government behind the Appalachians, or even the concepts of nationhood or government. However, in coming to Texas the Anglos did not discard their past, or culture.

They were never really asked to; although it was stipulated that they would become Roman Catholics, this was never enforced. The Mexican Church, smarting under its inability to collect tithes, supplied no clergy. Austin himself never became a Catholic, a fact known to and disregarded by the Mexican authorities who were themselves mostly Freemasons.

The colonists never learned Spanish. They quickly outnumbered the Hispanic population ten to one; they had no opportunity to learn the language, even if they had wanted to.

In most of the colonies scattered throughout the eastern part of Texas, the immigrant was permitted to live his own life and develop his property in accordance with his own wishes. Whether he was a prominent planter who brought capital in the form of slaves and tools, or one of the buckskin crowd — which Austin never favored — bent on subsistence farming along the Brazos, he could mark off his broad lands, hunt, fish, strive, raise cotton and sell it on foreign markets. He could get rich, or do nothing, letting his children and his hounds run wild in the stump-littered clearings around his cabin — so long as he bothered none of his neighbors.

The other side of the coin of this libertarian Eden was that no settler could expect much help from anyone. Neighbors banded together to protect each other against intruders; neighbors helped with roof-raising. Then and later, however, homesteads were usually many miles apart, and the good neighbor — and good citizen — was the one who took care of himself and his family competently on the frontier. There were no public institutions and no one wanted any; there was no organized law, no public assistance, no credit, and in fact, virtually no money.

Internal commerce was carried on by barter. The small farmers raised pigs and corn and traded for tools and bullets. They did without nails and made their own clothing. The planters lived a life style light-years removed from the borderers from upper Alabama and Tennessee. They barged cotton bales down to the Gulf, sold them abroad, and built up credits against which they imported goods and more slaves. Ninety-five percent of Texans, however, owned no blacks, and the free farmers were generally hostile both to the institution and its victims, wanting neither in their own territories.

Early Texas had neither banks nor jails. The few troublemakers were expelled, sometimes after a flogging; in this, Texas was much like early colonial America. Both types of residents, whether dirt farmers or lordly planters, had an aversion to banks and bankers and financial institutions — a prejudice that proved lasting.

Texas was thus the antithesis of a corporately conceived or organically organized society. From the first there were enormous differences in economic condition and social status among the colonists, but there was nothing approaching social or political hierarchy. The society was based upon land ownership. Every landholder was in determined theory a peer among equals, a member of a pure male democracy. Inevitably, the more enterprising and richer, the Groces and McNeels and others, gained prestige and an aura of leadership, but — and it is important to understand this — they were lords only upon their own land. The ideal and practice of society was one of social and political, but never economic equality, a notion that denizens of more organic societies have often found hard to comprehend.

It worked in Texas because for long years there was no shortage of land. Many came and departed, but those who stayed had no problem in securing extensive holdings — even if, as in many cases, the land could not be worked and was economically almost worthless.

This was of course a paradise that could not last, nor could it truly erect a new culture. It was a colony of a larger civilization, upon which it was dependent for niceties as well as many necessities. It also had to import teachers and clergymen, physicians, and even lawyers, all of whom collectively kept Texas firmly attached to the culture beyond the Sabine — just as in Kentucky they had inevitably imbedded the civilization of the Atlantic slopes. However, the Texans shaped the old society somewhat differently. This frontier did not quickly take on the trappings of the America of the nineteenth century; it much more resembled the wilderness of a hundred years earlier.

The Texas Revolution began for essentially the same reason that the American Revolution was carried out in 1776, and like the earlier revolt it was also very much an uprising against government itself. When Mexico, now frightened by a buffer that it began to see as a Trojan horse, moved to impose her authority over Texas, with customs, restrictions, laws, and finally, military garrisons planted among the colonists, explosion was inevitable. The rebellion involved a serious culture clash between an organic, essentially despotic society and the Anglo-American frontier — but it must be recalled that Texans lived willingly under Mexican sovereignty until the government became intrusive, and most substantial citizens opposed actual revolution to the last.

A social milieu had been made, and the Republic fostered it. Anxious to bring in more settlers, both as a safeguard and to increase the prosperity of the country, the Republic granted lands as lavishly as the Mexicans. The Texas Constitution, in a clause repeated in each successive State document, asserted the ideal that Texas was to be a Jeffersonian republic of freeholders. The "head right" — a term that still confuses out-of-state lawyers researching land titles — was a land grant available to each head of a family in Texas, whether established or newly arrived.

With an open frontier and an apparently endless array of lands to the west and south, this seemed a dream to be realized. Texas had created a society and state in which every man could become a landowner, however useless the land might be to him. This of course set up endless speculation — relatively few families held onto all their land — but it also created a mindset in which every Texan could envision himself as a petty emperor in his mini-empire.

The dream was propagated beyond the United States. German peasants, starving on painfully small plots in the years before industrialization, found the vision of 4,000 acres in Texas too much to resist. Thousands came, more than 30,000 in all in these years, not realizing that in some cases their grants lay in Comanche country, or in the stony hill country along the Edwards Plateau. They came, struggled, and put down roots in flinty soil, infusing Texas with German blood

— but not Germanic culture — over wide areas, and perhaps instilling in many Texans the European peasantry's feeling for the earth.

The dominant Texas mood and approach to the land, however, had nothing of a peasant's stolid attachment, nor anything like the Indian's mystic vision of nature. The urge was to master the land and carve out free holdings, on which the good citizen bothered no one and no one could bother him. When fences began to be built in Texas, whether of stone, wire, or wood, these became almost sovereign boundaries. Texan children were brought up to respect them, never cross them without permission, and even today many oldline Texans find the newcomers' disregard for private property and property lines, disconcerting and despicable.

The dream of universal landholding was almost realized. In 1860, four-fifths of all white Texans, most of the 400,000-plus native-born citizens, were landowners and self-employed. The dream of empire never extended to Negroes, the more than 180,000 slaves whom the colonists had carried into Texas with them, or who had been "sold South" in the years preceding the Civil War. Like all America in these years, this was a white republic only, although freed slaves could own land, and at least one former slave acquired properties that eventually made his family millionaires.

The dream was not destroyed by the War Between the States. Although "The War," as some still call it along the Brazos, ruined the planter class, as a class, new proprietors soon rose to take their lands. The great majority of Texans remained freeholders, and thousands more came to join them.

The reconstituted state, eager to rebuild and complete the conquest of the frontier, continued to sell, trade, or give away its public lands in the west so long as these lasted. Since Texas entered the Union as a sovereign nation, it retained title to all lands within its borders, a profound difference from the status of all other Western states. This, until the 1880s, continued to fuel land booms in West Texas, whether it traded land for

Confederate scrip or sold off an empire (the future XIT ranch) to raise money for a new State Capitol, and it continued until this form of capital was exhausted.

But the republic of freeholders was eroded and finally destroyed by the kind of nation the Civil War had made and the economy that followed it. Although most of the causes lay outside Texas, the effects, aggravated by periodic drouths, were more disastrous there than anywhere.

In the years just before the War, Texas had prospered. The standard of living rose; subsistence farming was becoming a thing of the past. People no longer built only cabins without nails or raised sod shanties on the plains; they put up substantial houses. And expectations rose with conditions and the slow entry of a monetary economy.

With the rails came banks and loans and credits and all the other amenities of civilization.

Meanwhile, the vast expansion of farming in the Plains states to the north as well as in Texas, the new rails going to market, and the invention of machinery such as reapers to harvest the prairies, caused a disastrous, long-term trend of falling crop prices. While the cotton-growing east survived, miserably, with its share-crop solution (the former large plantations were parceled out to tenants, both white and black, who worked small plots of ground for a share in the harvest) the west entered into economic catastrophe.

Hard-money policies and high tariffs, (which Texans had never known) however necessary to the erection of a powerful industrial nation in America, played havoc on the grain-farming frontier. In the nineteenth century the same forces that organized the United States into the first great "common market" also ruined the small farmer and rancher. They eroded the freedom and eventually the very existence of the small landowner in the fragile west, and not all the roaring protests of the People's, or Populist, Party (born in 1879 on the north-central Texas frontier) could stay the process.

Ironically, the same industrial civilization that permitted the frontier to advance with its repeating firearms, wire, rails, and windmills — and later, its development of power machinery to clear the scrub and break the plains and make the arid regions bloom with grain and cotton through the lavish application of new fertilizers — also destroyed that advance with hard money, tight credit, falling prices, and rate manipulation and speculation. If drouth or Indians didn't get the far-western farmer, the bank or storekeeper did.

This struggle went on all across the United States in the agrarian regions; it was never confined to Texas. But the lasting effects were greater in Texas. The land was depopulated faster, and there was no burgeoning industrial complex nearby to absorb the human detritus. Commodity prices were lower generally in 1895 than they had been in the Atlantic trading world in 1795, and by 1915 more than half of all Texans, white, black, or brown, had been forced into tenantry.

All the damage, certainly, was not caused by Eastern bankers and industrialists and railroads. Families lost lands for other reasons. Erratic nature and bad harvests conquered many. Some were indolent or lacked staying power. Some sold off lands in speculation. More were done in by the nature of the land itself, which resisted the tried and true techniques brought from other regions.

Across the 98th meridian, a whole population tried to advance in the teeth of nature, and nature defeated them.

One effect of this was that while upper-Midwestern cities were largely populated by foreign immigrants, the people streaming from the land for more than a century in Texas peopled their own cities. And this gave those cities a different outlook and ethos.

The defeated, many of whom retained at least some connection with the land, lost the battles; most, perhaps, have still not surrendered. The Texas cities themselves became nearly as atomistic as the frontier, never developing much of the neighborhood organization or mentality so prevalent in

Northern cities, in fact, never developing a true urban ethos through the present. Some observers believe they never will, because the cities are encompassed by the lands around them, still drawing on them in a continuing osmosis.

The marvel of this long misery, which lasted a century from the 1870s, is the tenacity with which the Anglo-Texan stuck with it. And for many, especially the survivors on the land — or those who may have moved to town but kept their holdings — it all transcended a mere business or economic struggle, just as the Cattle Kingdom somehow became more a way of life than an enterprise. It blended with the battles against the Indians, an eternal fight to take this land and hold it.

Texas became a land of big pastures and big farming operations, with tenant farmers themselves substantial operators. Agriculture was transformed, and transformed again with each new decade, and in the 1980s it is still undergoing painful transitions. But throughout the state, something that can only be called a landowner's ethos has survived, and it lives in the largest cities as well as in counties with a few thousand people.

The Anglos brought it with them, but Texas experience hammered it home in them. The land did not so much conquer Texans as it shaped them, in ways that the denizens of industrial societies find incomprehensible.

Opportunities and success were so long defined in Texas by landholding, and this so long defined society itself, that the drive is slow to die.

The land was peculiarly the source of all great wealth, and most wealth, as it still is today. First, there was the cotton money, long the most prestigious with its aura of plantation houses along the Brazos; then the great cattle baronies, creating a dozen millionaire families in some counties and small towns; the timber empires in the piney woods; finally the continuing oil bonanza (with its own booms and busts) that made richer many of the rich and erected new empires of its own.

The most successful Texans on the whole are those who, or whose families, held the land. The consciousness is deep among the survivors. In fact, it is often remarked that those who have retained their land remain as a presence in the community, while families who have sold or moved, whatever their eventual successes, have somehow "disappeared."

Through every change, boom or bust, the landowner, now land poor, now flush and powerful, has remained the ideal and the true apex of Texan society.

Most Texans were poor when they arrived in the state, and most remained poor. But the dream of private empire never died, and it works its way on the failures as much as the strong and successful. A vast number of Texans in their hearts admire the way the King Ranch does business. It has disputed with state and federal governments the right to build highways across its preserves, because they opened up its kingdom; it patrols its fences, guards its gates, regulates all who enter upon its sacred private grounds. No one is allowed in with rod or gun or alcoholic beverages, including those who work in the great refinery now within its confines, who sometimes feel they are passing onto sovereign soil. It is a mystic and mysterious empire, while at the same time a worldwide business enterprise. Yet it is and has usually been a good neighbor, giving much and asking only that it be left alone.

There is only one 825,000-acre *La Kineña*, but there are many petty "King Ranches" and corporations across the state. When a Texas rancher invites you to his "country," he is not referring to the United States, but to his private property wherever it may be.

This ethos is apparent in many ways. Texas has the strongest anti-trespass laws of any state. If a man's home is his castle under Anglo-Saxon law, a Texan's property is his kingdom. The notion of private right remains mentally unchanged since the eighteenth century, whatever newer notions and laws have done with it. A Scottish jurist recently remarked that if Britons want to understand the ethos of British law in the eighteenth century, they should study modern Texas. When property rights are modified or abridged, as in the striking down of Texas laws against picketing on private property, this has almost always been done by federal courts against the wishes of the dominant Texan viewpoint.

The private-property mindset had been destructive in some ways. The putting up and guarding of fence lines led to overgrazing on what had once been open range on which animals moved freely to the grass and water that was always somewhere on the plains. It has led to horrendous legal battles; in the nineteenth century Texas suffered from more litigation over land titles than any American state. Private property may still be destroyed for private, even ill-considered purposes, in Texas, and over the years the ecological damage to the native soil and grasses in the land of big pastures has been enormous.

It is hard to control pollution in Texas because of the fear of infringing on private rights. Houston is the only major metropolis in the nation that lives completely without zoning ordinances. With water, however, Texans have begun to accept controls, although every community itself is entirely responsible for providing this commodity for itself.

The view of private-property rights is often schizophrenic. Texans want the country to develop, grow, and more people to come, since all this increases prosperity and the value of the lands. Conversely, they resent crowding, or anyone trespassing on their rights. Recent polls show this clearly – and the question remains to be confronted in coming years.

Every Texan still feels the urge to own land, or real property; it is a far stronger urge, even in the cities, than to own a "piece of industrial America" or bonds. The so-called "prestige ranch" is acquired both by old families and newcomer corporation executives in San Antonio and Dallas. This country property, however uneconomic, is almost as important to wealthy urbanites as the country estate in eighteenth-century England, and it sells for comparably unrealistic prices. Texans need land, *their* land, the more the better, to satisfy some deep craving in their souls, even if the land no longer quite affords empire or independence or makes a man a king.

Those who left the land vanished, swallowed up in cities or in other states, and the generation of ex-sharecroppers and ranchers, lost in their atomistic suburbs, sense the fact with unease.

On the land, oil-rich or dirt-poor, the survivors take a precarious pride in their survival. More will go, more will come to replace them, but meanwhile, the immense land of Texas goes on forever, shaping the people at least as much as they will shape it in future generations.

CHAPTER IV

THE ECONOMY

Of all the keys to modern Texas, its economy is probably the least understood by contemporary Americans.

Texas is increasingly perceived as a rich state, filled with flamboyant, rich individuals whose money and influence are seen and felt in other parts. However, there is often so little understanding by outsiders of the forms and bases of this wealth that many who move to Texas seeking opportunity or employment suffer not only disappointment but also a form of culture shock.

Some newcomers expect Texas to be like Michigan or Pennsylvania, only less recession-prone; they are disillusioned, even somewhat angered, when they find out how different it is.

There has almost always been economic opportunity in Texas, and this holds as true in the 1980s as ever, even more so because of the growth of population and accelerating development. Texas still holds the "promise of empire." But the type of "empire" Texas offers the immigrant — although there is no longer a geographic frontier or land for the taking — has not essentially changed. For those prepared to do business, or who arrive with needed skills, or have the ability to acquire property, Texas compared to most states can be an entrepreneur's demi-paradise. Its economy is among the most lightly taxed and least regulated in the nation. In many parts of Texas, property is also relatively cheap by national standards. Trade-restricting associations are weak.

However, this is an economy that from beginning to present was based on the land, some form of real property and its products. Texas has not yet, and may never become a truly industrialized state, in which manufacturing — whether by traditional or new high technology — assumes prime importance and generates a complex infrastructure of managment, labor, government, research and education.

The economy of Texas was and is colonial in its basic structure. Texas produces, processes, and ships agricultural and mineral products to outside markets. For all the vaunted, thorny personal independence of the Texan, the Texas economy has always been utterly dependent upon the prices paid in national and world markets for its basic raw materials, whether cotton, cattle, or petroleum. And while Texas is among the leading producers of many things both in the nation and the world, it controls no markets — a factor behind much of the historic Texan hostility toward those who do control them.

While Texas is not so vulnerable to the recurrent ups and downs that affect all industrial economies, the state as a whole is terribly vulnerable to the booms and busts in agricultural and mineral markets. The 1970s, a time of industrial glut worldwide, was also a period of scarcity and artificially rising prices for agricultural and petroleum products. This allowed the Texan economy to bloom, fortunes to be made, and even the state government to pile up vast surpluses. But Texans have seen this same syndrome before, in a long history of the expansions and contractions of their markets.

Before the arrival of Anglo-Americans, Texas hardly had an economy. Beginning in the early eighteenth century, the province was colonized by Spain out of Mexico, with missions among the Indians, military garrisons, and mere handfuls of Hispanic settlers. The missions all eventually failed: Warlike aborigines such as the Comanches and Apaches would not permit the establishment of missions in their territories; the peaceful peoples like the Caddoans and Coahuiltecans were virtually exterminated by the infusion of European diseases such as smallpox.

Soldiers came and went; the missions were secularized; the small, hardy groups of Spanish colonists survived, mainly at San Antonio de Bexar, which became the capital of Spanish Texas. But the colony failed to thrive or grow, and the Hispanic population throughout the Mexican province was hardly more than 3,000 in all when Texas was opened to Anglo-American settlement.

The dearth of Spaniards or Mexicans willing to move to this raw frontier was one reason. Another cause was Spanish colonial policy, which barred the Texans from their natural trading partners in French Louisiana, making them dependent upon a distant Mexico that was separated by several hundred miles of virtual desert, and with which even simple communications were difficult in the ox-cart era.

Hispanic Texans practiced subsistence agriculture, a meagre life based upon goats and beans; they brought in the northern Mexican cattle culture and imbedded it firmly along the Rio Grande, but cattle remained more valuable for their hides than for their meat. This was a culture of great durability and considerable charm, but one basically devoid of growth or dynamism.

The Anglos arrived with vastly different cultural and economic imperatives. They were a people, for all their complete devotion to agriculture, of essentially mercantile drives. The majority of all Americans in Texas in the 1820s and 1830s were small farmers whose main activities were clearing land, putting in corn, and raising hogs. Their economy appeared largely self-sufficient and existed by barter. They built no towns. They were seemingly no more building a Texan civilization than the earlier Mexicans, and yet an enterprising class of major landholding capitalists developed rapidly along the river bottoms of southeastern Texas. The frontier fringes held more whites; they were rude and vigorous and politically important; but the planters created the first true Texan economy.

This was as colonial as early Virginia, and in fact the whole pattern of Texas development was much like that of the Southern seaboard in earlier centuries. The economy was based on large slave plantations; it had no use for cities or towns. The money crop, cotton, was barged downriver to the Gulf. Since reefs barred the mouths of all major Texas rivers, no natural harbors existed, and no port cities could develop. The cotton bales were lightered onto ships and sold abroad, either in Europe or the United States, mostly through New Orleans.

Eventually Galveston, on its island, arose as the major port and entrepot of Texas, and significantly, it remained the major Texas town for many years.

Because of the large expanses of rich coastal muck, all free or purchasable for a song, men with capital or credit could quickly create respectable incomes. They brought Texas into the Cotton Kingdom, and it differed from the Old South in 1860 only in that in Texas this economy was still expanding, still creating an enormous demand for more slave labor, although it had reached to within 150 miles of its western geographic limits.

Immediately upon the successful conclusion of the Texas Revolution substantial families began to erect mansion houses, a trend that received new impetus when Texas joined the Union and its future seemed assured. The Cotton Kingdom was the economic heart of both the Republic and State of Texas; its social patterns and politics dominated the more turbulent frontier.

Some of the largest planters were men of both regional and national importance, and it was not unusual even for a cotton-planting entrepreneur living in a rude house in new-cleared country to earn $5,000 in a single year — then an enormous sum in a state and nation in which hard money remained scarce. This opportunity drew substantial men as well as a horde of hunter-trappers to Texas, many of the former having moved westward from the eroded and exhausted areas ruined by exploitive tobacco and cotton agriculture in the older states.

The smaller farmers, restricted to land further inland that they themselves could work, had less access to foreign markets and did less well. However, in the flush cotton-boom era preceding the Civil War, the whole region prospered according to the expectations of the times.

This economy, however, was completely "colonial" in all its aspects. Those who earned money abroad, bought abroad. Fine houses rose both in Galveston and along the rich river bottoms. Every luxury, from fine boots and horses to ice, could be procured in Texas — but it was all brought in from outside, just like the Colt revolvers that were "winning the frontier."

This is a pattern very old in human history, reaching back far beyond the settlement of the Americas into ancient times. Greece and Rome played the role of "developed" economies for the outliers in Europe and around the Black Sea, shipping wine and oil and civilized artifacts in return for lumber and grain. The viability of human slavery in Texas was akin to the slavery originally fostered among the outliers in ancient times, the serfdom that was instituted in Eastern Europe to supply Western markets, and the black servitude that had its vast recrudescence in the Western Hemisphere. This was part of the history and pattern of the whole American South — but with a certain difference.

If slavery had long become uneconomic in the American North, by 1860 it was also losing much of its drive and rationale in places like Virginia — where, increasingly uneconomic as an institution, it was defended largely as an emotional reaction to the moral attacks of the Abolitionists. In Texas neither the economic nor the moral argument ever really arose — until Emancipation, slaves actually remained far more valuable, in money terms, than land. There was a voracious need and demand for labor to exploit the land commercially — and had not politics intervened, the institution would have lasted along the Texas Gulf Coast for at least another generation.

Cotton, if not the Cotton Kingdom of the Old South, survived the War Between the States. It remained the economic basis for most of Texas. Many of the "old families" were destroyed financially and socially by the loss of their human capital. However, the sharecrop solution — the institution of a new form of land tenantry by which the former slaves and eventually a large part of the poorer white population, were held on the land — actually increased cotton acreage and production, which continued to be exported to European or New England mills as before.

The Cattle Kingdom, which Texans inherited from the Mexicans, adapted to Northern industrial markets hungry for beef, and spread across the entire West. It captured the fancy of both Texans and the world in the latter nineteenth century — but it never engaged lives, labors, and fortunes, meagre as most of them were, as cotton did. Texas had become first in cotton production, and first it would remain, although the old élan was gone.

At first the cattle business involved no more than rounding up the semi-wild cattle that had proliferated, untended, on the Nueces bottomlands, and driving them to Kansas railheads.

This forged a new link between enterprising people on the frontier and the developing industrial marketplace. For all its glamor — the open range, the abortive cowboy culture, with its own loyalties, loneliness, manhood rites and version of the code duello — Western ranching was essentially a money-making business, managed by very hard-headed men. It was extremely important to Texas, not only because of the Yankee dollar cattlemen brought back to a state stagnating from war and occupation, but because it provided a new frontier and an outlet from the funks and despairs of Texan defeat and the degradation of the old cotton-raising society. It was even good for the nation; as Walter Prescott Webb wrote, it let North and South meet again at Abilene and do business together.

Dependent upon the new Northern markets, the Texas west was also dependent upon the distant industrial technology. Beef and hides paid for wire and windmills and Winchester rifles as what had been an opportunity became an established stock-raising business. Texas "cattle barons," the men who emerged, sometimes seemingly from nowhere, to organize big ranches and move thousands of beeves to market, were never anything like the *hacendados* or *latifundistas* of Mexico, or the aristocratic landowners on the European continent. Like cotton planters, they were a form of businessman. Cool and pragmatic, some took risks in Indian country but most of them avoided these until the Army solved the problem. Charles Goodnight, for example, bypassed the dangerous Comanche ranges, moving into the safer terrain of New Mexico, only entering the Texas Panhandle from the west when the Comanche threat was obviously waning. These men endured the hardships of the country and the rigors of the trail drive as a part of business — and the best and most far-seeing of them invested their earnings in acquiring land and better breeding stock — for the open range and the supply of range-bred longhorns was soon exhausted. By the 1880s ranching had become so much a business as opposed to a way of life that cowhands, now too numerous and feeling oppressed by the changes in the country, sometimes tried to strike — but those little known and scattered labor actions were doomed to failure on the former frontier.

Like the earlier cotton capitalism of East Texas, the West Texas cattle business drew men and money from far away. A great deal of investment came from the British Isles, bringing famous breeds and scattering a few Scottish names and tiny

Anglican churches in remote places in the vast semi-arid wilderness.

And like the cotton trade, ranching involved the raising and shipment of agricultural products to distant markets, both domestic and foreign, whether by dusty trail, railroad cattle car, or in later years by modern semitrailer.

Sheep and goat raising also came to Texas in the years following the Civil War, again creating a large enterprise in a similar fashion. Once the Merino sheep and Angora goat became established in the Hill Country west of San Antonio, the disgust of cattlemen notwithstanding, that city became the wool and mohair capital of the nineteenth-century world.

As rails opened up Eastern markets for the West, they also made it easier to exploit the great pine forests near the Louisiana border. The Texas timber empires, again a "semi-feudal" economic pattern in which strong men put together powerful companies and vigorous exploitive enterprises, followed in the paths of the earlier kingdoms. Lumber, like cotton and cattle, left Texas to meet a foreign demand, leaving its own forms of devastation behind.

Pecans, peanuts, and petroleum, all the products which the huge regions of Texas came to provide in such enormous quantity, were merely newer versions and expansions of the same colonial pattern. They were all based on the land, came from the land, and largely enriched the possessors of the land — primarily those owners of large holdings who could develop and often devastate the land for the sake of profit. The small cotton farmers, the homesteading types brought out by railroads, along with transplanted European peasants who approached agriculture as a way of life, in all their countless thousands across Texas, fared much worse economically. They rarely got ahead and were defeated by bad weather cycles and bad market years, both of which became endemic by the 1880s.

The tendency of economic development in Texas was that both large and small agricultural enterprises started together, with the smaller in the vast majority. The frontier was harsher than other regions; the ratio of failures higher. A universal pattern — as true in eighteenth-century England as nineteenth and twentieth-century Texas — followed: the large grew larger. This was not so much a matter of the little fish being swallowed up by the bigger fish in aggressive competition as it was the simple survival of the stronger. It was a natural process arising out of stresses and bad times in the absence of any social legislation to prevent it.

The large ranch, the large landholding, obscured in most of eastern Texas by the widespread adoption of tenant farming — thousands of acres owned by one person or family might be scattered across the bottoms and parceled out to many different operators — inevitably became the norm for most of Texas.

Geography had as much to do with this over the years as economic conditions. Over much of Texas in this century and the last, agriculture was attempted in areas where soils or climate were unsuited for it; even in years of excellent markets no one could — or can — make a decent living from small acreages on which, by world standards, yields are very low. Scale, as well as economies of scale, is demanded, Precarious rainfall has always made dry-farming hazardous over any period of years. Even prior to the Civil War, when most Texans lived, or tried to live on small subsistence farms, there was no real future for those with only forty acres and a mule — a fact that the economic developments of the last half of the century drove home with vast attendant agrarian misery.

Landholdings had to be of a certain size to survive as viable operations. The Spanish recognized the need for larger holdings, especially for stock-raising, a fact that Anglo-Saxon politics and law never quite grasped. In semi-arid regions, huge expanses of territory are necessary to support even a few animals. Much "good East Texas graze" needs twelve acres to feed a single cow, and the ratio rises sharply as one goes westward.

While the smallholder stayed poor, the large landowner did not necessarily become rich. Ranches that seemed princely on the map, before petroleum was discovered under them, would not support a family in style, or anything approaching the affluence of an Eastern industrialist. The cattleman's tradition was a frugal one, and traces of this still exist.

Meanwhile, in whole regions of Texas profitable agricultural development was not carried out until well into this century. The capital and techniques of nineteenth-century settlers were not sufficient to attack either the Rio Grande Valley or the vast Panhandle and South Plains regions. In the south, not only did brush have to be cleared, the farming of that cleared land required extensive investment in irrigation and drainage projects. The Valley could be developed only by large land companies with the necessary capital and cheap labor, the latter factor offsetting the area's disadvantage of being distant from its markets. Northern and Midwestern developers provided the first, neighboring Mexico the second, giving the Valley its "feudal" aspect, which was more the fault of geography than any human intent.

The Plains could be farmed profitably only by large economies of scale. Agriculture only began to supplant grazing with the appearance of heavy power machinery — at first, steam tractors to till mile-long furrows, then pumps to draw up deep artesian water, and the development of fertilizers to correct alkalinity in the soils. Agriculture, gradually extended to its natural limits in Texas, and perhaps beyond, was halted finally by an acute shortage of water. The nine million acres under irrigation comprise only a third of Texas farmlands, but they are the most productive — and this acreage cannot be increased further.

As the aquifers in west Texas continue to be depleted by pumping, the high cost of production as well as the exhaustion of water resources will undoubtedly return huge areas to pasture lands, if not in this century, certainly in the next.

With a climate given to harsh extremes, mediocre soils

(compared to those of the great grain-growing regions of the world) and relatively poor yields per acre, even large-scale agriculture in Texas has always been precarious – a high-roller's risk in which the weak or unlucky continually are eliminated.

The other factor of high risk in Texas agriculture, its vulnerability to commodity prices and export markets, is the same today as it was during the years in which falling prices or disappearing markets drove thousands of nineteenth-century smallholders into tenantry and, when the European war cut off Texas beef exports, drove thousands of cattlemen into bankruptcy in 1915. Inconstant weather, especially recurring drouths, may have done more overall damage to Texas farmers and ranchers than fluctuating economic conditions. In any event, it is safe to say that whenever these two factors combine – as they did in the 1880s, in 1915, during the dustbowl years of the 1930s, and the long dry spells of the 1950s – the effect has been devastating. The risk of dependence on export markets is ever present. In the 1980s, 30 percent of the total agricultural production in Texas goes overseas. These foreign markets are vital, but Texans do not control them.

Because few Texans are directly involved in agribusiness – less than 5 percent compared to more than 30 percent in 1940 – its importance to the economy of the state is frequently overlooked. However, the value of farm assets totals three-fourths of the assets of all state and national banks in Texas. Every dollar of agricultural sales pours three and a half dollars into the economy; and the multiplier effect, with a vast amount of Texas manufacturing really consisting of the processing of agrarian products, is enormous, more than $33 billion per year.

Texas is the number-one producer of cattle, cotton, and sorghum; it ranks among the top ten states as a producer of some sixteen commodities, and second in terms of agricultural sales.

Oil, which made most of the twentieth-century great fortunes and which became the driving force behind the economy, financing not only 30 percent of government but a vast array of other enterprises, co-exists nicely with agriculture. It made no real change in either economic or social patterns. Mineral wealth is only another resource of the land, another Texas product to be exported. And although perfectly natural distinctions and disagreements arose between ranchers with oil wells on their ranges and those who had none, oil itself enjoyed and continues to suffer from cycles of boom and bust.

The great oil discoveries of the 1930s in East Texas created an oversupply in a depressed American economy. State government, in what was then a radical step, instituted production controls through proration. Texas, with some success, controlled the amount of petroleum that could be pumped and shipped. Again, after the boom World War II years, the industry entered hard times as the United States' market turned increasingly to cheaper Arabian crude. For many years in the 1950s and 1960s, Texas wells were limited to eight days' production per month. Meanwhile, federal price regulation of natural gas stultified that entire industry.

This very uncertain situation was resolved, ironically, by the Organization of Petroleum Exporting Countries, or OPEC. This cartel created artificial scarcity and soaring prices. Had Texas been an independent nation it could have been a major member of OPEC; in any case, the state benefitted as much as Saudi Arabia, especially after the federal government finally deregulated domestic petroleum.

Money in all modern economies has an enormous multiplying effect. A mere $3 billion in direct agricultural sales is magnified more than ten times in its diffusion and impact; similarly, the $15 billion Texas earned from petroleum flushed through the whole state economy explosively. By the late 1970s the expansion of exploration and drilling was pouring new money into many areas of the state (except East Texas), creating new jobs in all energy-related fields — and spreading far beyond that, enriching the operators of motels and cafes in dozens of dusty little towns. All business prospered from this cascade of cash and credit.

Oil and gas, along with the flush times for most Texas commodities, had a tremendous impact on the Texas economy. From 1975 to 1979, business incorporations increased 25 percent each year, twice the national average and a third greater than in any other Sunbelt state. By the early 1980s, new business incorporations approached 50,000 annually, a figure that dazzled the nation and heightened the Texas economic mystique of a region on the move, a recession-proof miracle in the midst of an aging and declining American economy.

The 1970s, in fact, were years of remarkable growth. By 1980, Texas had grown from fifth to second in total retail sales among the states, to seventh in value added from manufacturing, to first in capital investment, to third in farm income, and to third in total income and bank deposits – behind only California and New York.

It remained first in total mineral production and had the lowest unemployment rate of any state.

But it was not seen, even by many Texans, that this economic miracle depended on more than the business climate and entrepreneurial energy of the people. It rested primarily upon the extraordinary demand and high prices for Texas' basic products of petroleum, food, and fibers during the decade. The new prosperity could not be quickly translated into solid new economic structures or lasting employment, no more than in Mexico or the Persian Gulf States. And many smart Texas businessmen never expected it to last. Oldtimers in the oil business, especially, smiled coldly while they watched newcomers and half the stockbrokers in Dallas get "into oil" by forming new exploration and drilling firms, and bankers who had never seen the 1950s waxed enthusiastic over smoke. Those "in the know" waited for the bust – which began in 1981 and by early 1982 was in full swing.

Oil demand and prices fell; meanwhile, there was an over-supply of nearly everything that served the oil patch, from pipe to people.

This was always, like cotton, cattle, and Texas real estate, a high-rollers' game. But the hordes of new oil people marched as bravely into the West as the homesteaders of old. While fortunes *were* made, construction boomed, and businessmen flocked to Texas like salespeople gathering in Arabia, the oil patch proved to be as slippery as any earlier economic frontier.

Significantly, oil production actually peaked in Texas in 1972 – a year before OPEC made it a new world. All the new holes punched in Texas soil, all the new exploration, the new recovery methods, the re-opening of formerly uneconomic fields have not brought production back to the level of that year.

Oil in the 1980s is a vast but flat or even declining enterprise. The Oil Empire is still enormous, and like the Cotton and Cattle Kingdoms, it would have its heyday and survive – but like them it would remain precariously dependent upon declining resources and price structures which no Texan can control.

Unlike Mexicans and some other peoples, Texans have never regarded their natural resources as a sort of patrimony. They are to be exploited and not hoarded, and Texans are impatient with anything that gets in the way of the exploitation. The Texas anger, expressed in bumper stickers such as the famous "Let the Yankee Bastards Freeze in the Dark" was not directed against the export to or use by Yankees of Texas energy – which supplied 38 percent of the national total – but what most Texans regarded as unjustified Northern and Eastern interference in the marketplace, to keep prices low.

The War Between the States may be over even in the Brazos bottoms, but some wars never end.

In recent years Texas' economy has inevitably grown much closer to, and much more akin to the American economy as a whole. Fueled by the energy boom, this happened especially in the 1970s, as the population and economy expanded rapidly. Trade of all kinds swelled enormously, as did manufacturing in general, while professional services doubled within two decades.

Transportation, communication, public utilities, finance, insurance, and real estate now add more to the $138 billion Gross State Product than agribusiness and mining, and services add as much as oil.

Texans now make their living in most of the same ways, as do the inhabitants of other major states. The same retail chains and fast-food stands deface the landscape; the same architectural styles prevail; the same national fads sweep Texas as they parade from coast to coast.

However, there are fundamental differences between Texas and the major industrial states. Although a quarter of Texas workers are employed in manufacturing, this is industry with a distinctly Texas coloration. Half of all industrial production is devoted to non-durable goods, and a great part of all manufacturing is in the processing of Texas farm and ranch products or minerals, whether packing beef or cracking petroleum. Much is also in support of purely local enterprise, such as cement plants, or the single steel mill which made drilling pipe and fell on hard times with the decline of drilling.

Texas' economy is not so diversified as that of California or New York, nor so complex, because it never developed a full industrial base. In the 1980s there are only a few pockets of truly industrial areas, mainly centered around Houston-Baytown and Dallas. In the 1970s when the major crisis of the American economy centered in heavy manufacturing, autos, steel, and durable goods, this actually proved to be an advantage for Texas and other Sunbelt states. Although Texas manufacturers were and are in no sense recession-proof, and unemployment in many Texas industries increased, this had less real effect on the total state economy than in the heavily industrialized states.

During 1982, for example, retail sales remained at high or even rising levels across the state, and while unemployment rose and many businesses failed, more new businesses were still being established than going broke.

Texas enterprise, meanwhile, despite popular mythology, is overwhelmingly small in nature. Ninety percent of all natural gas and petroleum production companies employ twenty persons or less, and the same is true of 85 percent of all gas and petroleum exploration firms. The great majority of all the electronic, computer and data processing, and information technology businesses in Texas hire no more than a dozen employees — in fact 80 percent of the work force is employed in firms with an average of twelve on the payroll. For all its "giant" image, Texas is not dominated by corporate giants.

There are few huge industries under one corporate roof which play a dominant role in Texas cities and towns. The oil business is gigantic over all, but it is divided into thousands of relatively small operators — and this, conversely, is what gives the industry such widespread, pervasive economic power and political power. The reality, and above all the spirit, of Texas enterprise has remained entrepreneurial in this century. Texans do not automatically confuse corporate bureaucracies such as General Motors, or the huge multinational oil companies, with businessmen in general. The driving force, and the basic power, of enterprise in Texas has always come from individuals, mostly men (because of lingering Southern cultural influences) who came to the frontier to forge a personal "empire," even if this consisted only of an insurance agency or a hardscrabble farm.

Because of this spirit, the lack of heavy industry and heavy industrial development, and the smallness, in people terms, of most businesses, business society has remained relatively simple in its outlines. It is basically two-tiered, owners and employees, with lines sharply drawn and with few layers of management in-between.

Primary and secondary jobs abound, because most Texas enterprise raises or pumps a product, makes a product, processes a product, and sells a product – drawing upon only such services, such as finance, as this requires. There is a great array of technical jobs, because even the most basic production such as agriculture is now solidly based upon machinery, chemistry, animal biology, and entomology. In every industry from petroleum to communications Texas absorbs thousands of specialists of all kinds, many if not most of which still come from outside.

Texas education, while expanding rapidly, has never produced enough technicians or professionals – except lawyers – to service the economy or provide the amenities of modern life.

During the 1970s boom times, Texas needed large numbers of construction workers, but not many unskilled or semiskilled laborers. This is an economy which still does not, and probably never will provide many blue-collar opportunities.

Like oil, gas, and agriculture, most Texas enterprise, including the newer high-technology industries sprouting across the Southwest, is capital rather than labor-intensive. Nothing like the historically peculiar structure of high-paying employment for essentially unskilled, assemblyline labor, aided and abetted by unionism in the American industrial belt, has ever existed or is being created now in Texas. The increasingly high-technology industry of the future is, in fact, more geared to the Texas norm than that of the aging mass-production heavy industries of the North and Midwest.

There are few aggregations of industrial workers. The Texas workplace, both city and town, is characterized by owner-operators, technical types (such as geologists, chemists, engineers), clerical personnel, and janitorial staff. Where light manufacturing or processing exists, it does not provide high pay for basically unskilled labor. Many firms also prefer to use consultant services rather than in-house employees, and many services are provided by independent contractors. This gives most Texas communities, and even the larger cities, an infrastructure quite different from most American industrial towns.

It follows that, although great wealth can be created in such an infrastructure, it is not necessarily widely diffused, and labor unions are relatively few and weak. Labor is mostly unorganized, and labor organizations lack economic and political power. It further follows that labor has no artificial clout in the marketplace, and wages and salaries generally remain lower than the national average – although per capita income is slightly above the national norm.

While construction jobs proliferated in many areas of Texas during the 1970s and early 1980s, hourly pay for construction crew members in Dallas, for example, was frequently only a third of prevailing rates in states such as Pennsylvania or Michigan, which are both highly unionized.

In this kind of economy public employment is less and less well-paid, because it does not rest on a large industrial tax base. Although it grew enormously, expanding tenfold in about ten years from 1972 – financed without raising taxes because of the huge inflow of revenue from the oil boom – there is still nothing in Texas, on a state or local level, comparable to the administratively expensive governments of California, Massachusetts, or New York.

This has not always been seen too well outside Texas. In the very years that some of the greatest fortunes have been made in the past, many laborers left Texas for other states.

Good jobs, in fact, never really existed on the old frontier, for frontier-type economies create opportunities for enterprise and skilled services, not necessarily for ordinary labor. The Texans who shaped the dominant economic patterns of the state have always filled the jobs they created by their actions as conveniently and as inexpensively as possible: with slaves, sharecroppers, and flotsam of drifting youth as cowboys, defeated men, and imported Mexican workers. And in a real sense, old socio-ecnomic patterns persist in today's industrial sector.

Cultural patterns resist change, even as economies change rapidly. The Japanese translated feudal structures into modern industrial corporations; the English, to their economic detriment, instilled the dominant ideals of the aristocracy into the heirs of their middle-class entreprenuers and industrialists.

In modern Texas enterprise, there are residues of the old plantation owner-overseer-slave and the rancher-foreman-hired-hand structures.

Men could and did continually become rich in Texas; they still do — but rarely by working for someone else, and even more rarely, by working up in an organization. Texas was created by men who went for the main chance, whether at Spindletop or San Jacinto. The industrious and enterprising built their own empires, and this ethos still infuses the business community.

The economy has always produced propertied and very rich Texans, whether they inherit land or erect a new utility or petroleum giant. But the prominence of these wealthy few has long obscured the pertinent fact that most Texans are not rich, and historically, most have been quite poor. In 1929, the per capita state income was only 68 percent of the national average. In the World War II boom years this rose to 93 percent, then slipped back to 83 percent by 1963. After the flush times of the 1970s it reached the national average for the first time — in real terms, it is a bit better, due to lower living costs and lower taxation in Texas. However, the "rich" state of Texas ranks seventh in average income, behind Nevada, California, Florida, Illinois, and even Delaware.

And per capita incomes are flawed as a measuring device because of the historic disparity between the value of property and labor. Texas teachers, for example, remain among the lowest paid in the nation. The borderlands communities, Brownsville-Harlingen-McAllen, Laredo, and even El Paso and San Antonio, consistently rank as the bottom metropolitan areas — with poverty pockets resembling the Third World — in the United States.

Until relatively recent times in this century, the minority populations, brown and black, were largely outside the money economy.

Yet Texas wealth stands out. There is a very rich community scattered across the state, and it is particularly noticeable in the modern metropoli such as Houston and Dallas, where the economy is closest to the national norm. One reason is that Texas money is largely new money, therefore more flamboyant and more vigorous. It is also personally held, not tied up in estates, or administered through trust funds. Corporate wealth is more often than not wielded by a single person or a single family, rarely a board of corporate directors. Only very recently have rich Texans overcome an innate distaste for such things as bank-administered money, or family trust funds, and this has been spurred less by changing attitudes than by federal taxes.

Texas money often has great impact, because it can move swiftly. If a Texan, or group of Texans, decide to buy the Bank of California (as some did) they can put it all together on a weekend, tell their lawyers what they want to do — and leave the hired specialists to handle the details.

Thus while there are far more millionaires and wealthy families on both the west and east coasts, these are not so much in the public eye, nor do they make as much impression in the marketplace.

The opportunistic strain, born of cotton and cattle and oil booms and busts and vast speculations in real estate, has not died. Dallas, as a city, raised itself by its own boot straps from the prairie. A key factor early in this century was the exodus of the major insurance companies from the state, caused by a law that required them to invest their funds in Texas. By the time the national corporations had rethought, enterprising people in Dallas had erected a large local insurance industry.

In the same way, Texas bankers pursued vision and ambition in the teeth of the state law that made branch-banking illegal, until the floodgates were broken by the ingenious device of holding companies.

If the Texas economy is the last refuge of the jackleg — as is often said — it is also one of the last refuges of the entrepreneur in North America. Texans have shown others the way in enterprises ranging from jewelry, airlines, groceries, to fried chicken franchising, as well as oil.

Characteristically, as the statistics show, even the largest enterprises tend to remain small and closely held and operated, especially when viewed on a comparative national or world scale. A Hughes Tool Company remains a personal business. However, with time, entrepreneurs die, or businesses grow too large and follow the national pattern of falling into the hands of professional management. And even in Texas this tends, as with all "mature" American business enterprise, to stultify it and make it grow stale and less competitive. As Braniff became a local and a lesser national disaster, and as other companies such as Texas Instruments grow senile, there is worry in Texas that the state's economy may pass into the hands of corporate bureaucrats disguised as businessmen who, however capable, are rarely as smart, daring, gut-tough, or personally rich as the men who built it.

Significantly, the huge petroleum companies that dominate the world's oil business were not founded in Texas, although many fueled themselves there, and they have always been a presence. Texans never produced a Standard Oil, no more than an Honorable East India Company. This is not the traditional Texan style. The Texan pattern is big man, faceless firm — some people never heard of the corporate name — never big companies with faceless men.

Many of the biggest operators in fact despise the modern American corporation, with all its accoutrements and hangers-on. Out of their culture and biases, most Texans prefer to think of corporations as legal limited liability devices, or a means to avoid taxation, hardly ever as social or economic institutions with a life of their own.

The average Texan tends to be outraged by the newer sort of liberal thinking, so prevalent among some Northern educated elites, that believes that corporations should be publicly owned. It runs, of course, against the grain of private property worship. But there is also another reason: Not being dominated by giant corporate industries in which, as in the Army, all ranks are hired hands, the Texan no more understands the problems and abuses of such a society than a country without priests can understand anti-clericalism.

This feeling is not antisocial; it is rather asocial, a hand-me-down from the simpler society of the American frontier. And it is not confined only to rich men or entrepreneurial types. The true-born Texan remains as suspicious as his ancestors were of most associations with corporate overtones or collective social significance, including labor unions. Even when a Texan joins a union in his personal economic interest, he may continue secretly to despise it.

In the same way, many Texan academics hate the academic bureaucracy even while they manipulate it. The goal in the inner heart of most Texans is to resist engulfment in the corporate society. It is a losing battle in a state and world with fewer and fewer places for independent persons — but Texans still make a virtue of values some non-Texans see as failings.

This trait, more felt than rationalized or articulated, still influences Texans' actions, and it should be understood by all who deal with Texans.

True or not, the lesson Texans take from their economic experience is this: The person of enterprise sometimes succeeds, while others come to live on his leavings or by his beneficence. It may be a harsh view, but it seems to be the way the world of Texas is, and as most Texans believe, the way it should be.

The Texas economy, then, for all its seeming complexity of trades and jobs and business opportunities, shows some very simple strains, and it is dominated by some very simple ideas.

It is based primarily on the exploitation of property, and it is as "colonial" in its framework as that of any South American country, for all its enormous differences in Anglo culture, ethos, acquired wealth, work ethic, efficiency, and organization. But it is not backward in any organizational or technical sense — the history of the cotton, cattle, timber, oil, or aviation and insurance and banking empires is a story of the seizure and adaptation and use of the latest industrial technology of the times to Texas opportunities.

It is an economy less of organizations than of people, usually hard-driving, essentially pragmatic men.

It is ruled less by ideas or ideologies than gut instinct — doing what comes naturally, as Texans say.

It has thrown up both a splendid edifice of ambitious entrepreneurs in nearly every line of enterprise and an efficient substructure of good farmers and ranchers — as aware of the *Wall Street Journal* and price trends as they are of the latest weather report — oil field technicians, and all the services required to support and exploit the production and processing of Texas products. Cotton creates cotton gins and compresses, cotton brokers, and farm equipment dealers, truckers, entomologists, and fertilizer and seed salesmen. The other great land-based enterprises do the same, from boot-makers to cement plants. The system creates bankers because they are necessary, and lawyers, for the same reason, but with some degree of reluctance.

It is a practical economy at base: People must produce something, or service those who do.

It has exported and is still exporting its excellences and techniques across the world. Texas drillers taught their skills to both Mexicans and Venezuelans. When a North Sea well is put down, its drilling platform — a Texas tower — more than likely has been made in Texas. Texans operate it initially, and if there is a fire, a Texas troubleshooter will be flown in from wherever his last assignment took him, whether from Scotland or Indonesia. Even the jargon of Arabian oil fields is "Texan."

The Japanese have shown little interest in American industrial techniques in recent years — the flow has been the other way around — but they arrive regularly to study Texan agrarian technology. Texan stock raisers exist in symbiosis with most of the grazing areas of the world, and great Texan-owned ranches operate on several continents.

It is an economy that creates practical education. Texas produces superb geologists, agricultural experts, and engineers, as well as lawyers. Texas meanwhile has always imported most of its doctors, social-service technicians, and clergymen. And 90 percent of the basic research that supports Texas enterprise is still farmed out, and is done in places less driven by ceaseless action, where ideas can germinate and thrive.

Texas is an economy, growing richer, that now consumes increasing amounts of imported culture, from great art to music and antiques. It creates little fine art of its own, but support for the arts is growing, and it is reasonable to assume that Texas, in time, will create its own artistic tradition.

Texas is an economy that would be stultified and stagnant without both its soil and ethic. Without the soil, there would be no initial infusion of money to act as multiplier, both in agribusiness and oil; without the ethic, Texas might easily be another Argentina — a land, in fact, more richly endowed in many ways.

Texas is an economy utterly dependent upon the outside industrial and technical world, for most of its artifacts and new techniques as well as its conveniences and luxuries. It has always had to import all its Colts and Cadillacs. And it is an economy whose supporters can easily come to resent such a situation, especially when outsiders attempt to control the markets so vital to Texans' economic well-being.

Not just oil men resented Yankee efforts to control oil; virtually every native-born Texan did, and still does, even though the vast majority, to their regret, will never own a drop of it.

It is an economy which to date has not produced a truly industrial, or managerial society. Its myriad enterprises are not yet enclosed in those private American bureaucracies that pass for businesses in most older states. What Peter Drucker called the "managerial revolution" passed Texas by or rather, never arrived.

The entrepreneurial ethic, in America both extravagantly praised but also in practice bitterly despised, is alive and well in Texas. The maker of economic empires — who may be personally hated — remains a cultural hero. Not accidentally, Texas retains perhaps the best "business climate" in the nation, in the sense that taxes on business do not oppress, unions do not dictate, and people on some public payroll do not constantly harass — and the public interest, which few Texans can define, does not intrude.

This economy is in no sense made; it is not finished or mature. The land is no longer limitless. Resources such as water and petroleum are dwindling. No matter how many Texans may emotionally reject the fact, growth in many of the old areas and industries is blocked. But the land is still immense, still relatively underpopulated. Although some forms of wealth will run out, the Texan faith — the Western, pioneer faith — is that others are still waiting to be found.

By the 1980s, with the stagnating if not ending of the oil boom and the bite of worldwide recession upon most Texas enterprise, it sould be clear to all that Texas is not a magic land. The tragic conclaves of displaced Northerners, living in trucks and autos parked on fields outside Houston and other Texas cities, the new Okies of this generation who came seeking the new California, perhaps, attested to that. But Texas is still a sometimes magnificent, sometimes harsh frontier. After each successive boom and bust the survivors become richer and more assured.

Texas still possesses an economy of great promise and vast potential, but it also has a tragic potential for those who dare the eternal American frontier. Texas is no place for economic refugees fleeing from some lost paradise and seeking a promised land of boundless and automatic opportunity.

It is, however, a place of limitless horizons for those who understand and can master its imperatives.

CHAPTER *V*

THE SOCIETY

THE economy of Texas has moved closer to the national norm; 80 percent of Texans have left the land since 1940 and live in cities; a quarter of the Texan work force is engaged in some sort of manufacturing. On the surface, the Texas social scene seems to be a principal tributary of the American mainstream.

But there are subtle and not-so-subtle differences beneath the common plasticized surfaces, especially between Texas and the industrialized states.

For example, it is not uncommon for Texas corporate executives of national standing and top-rung remuneration to introduce or identify themselves as hired hands. The statement is neither coy, satirical, nor self-demeaning. It clarifies something that is still important in Texas, where even a corporate superstar, if he does not own his company, may stand in the position similar to that of a prime athlete vis-à-vis the owner of the New York Yankees.

While the tendency of Texans living outside the state to form "Texans in Exile" or other such nostalgic groups is well known, outlanders who have moved to Dallas and other Texas communities in recent years have formed "Damn Yankee" and similar organizations. This is only partly satirical; it is also a psychic and cultural protective measure frequently taken by many immigrants who feel they need reassurance in an alien society.

Meanwhile, in a pattern at least as old as King David's soldier Uriah the Hittite, who became more Hebrew than the Hebrews, many newcomers to Texas turn into the most ardent converts of all, even surpassing natives in their devotion to "Texanism."

Such things point up a fact that many Americans fail to recognize — and some will deny or resent — that the boundaries of Texas are not mere administrative lines of jurisdictional convenience drawn on the map of the United States. Texas society still shows profound differences from those of New York or California. And these are not confined to the quaint small towns or the backwoods; they flourish in Dallas, Houston, and San Antonio.

Many of the differences are not unique to Texas; in some way or other most of them are found across the region now called the Sunbelt. But just as Texas is bigger, nearly everything in Texas becomes exaggerated and commands attention.

Texas society springs in part from its economy — but only in part. Birth, place, and race, and perhaps religion, come before occupation in its processes of self-identification. When a person in Texas asks immediately, "What do you do?" instead of "Where are you from?" the odds are high that he or she is an outlander who lacks a deep-seated personal sense of place and belonging.

Texas society also springs from its people, their ethic and culture, their ideals and mythology, and their history, which includes the way urbanization and industrialization have come about. If all industrial societies inevitably followed the same course in societal and cultural terms, then the whole world would be like nineteenth-century England, and modern Frenchmen would resemble modern Russians. It is a truism in Texas that, except in and around the industrialized enclaves of Houston and Dallas, the state has never joined the "industrial society" as that concept is recognized nationally. But the actual truth is that the United States has been busy creating several "industrial" societies. There is the industrial society of the Northern manufacturing states, the industrializing society of the South, and the modern society of Texas, all of which have similarities but are not the same.

Texans *have* created a modern society during the long struggle upward from the frontier. But they have not surrendered everything in the process, especially the ancient, independent, inherently asocial consciousness of their ancestors who first rejected European society and then forged their own culture on the Southern frontiers. Texas intellectuals, noticeably, are almost never marxist, determinist, or collectivist in their world views. The very notions are repugnant, not intellectually, but culturally. Thinking Texans with average incomes may hate rich men and worry about the "interests" that politicians love to lambaste — but they also tend to hate "socialism" more.

This culture has always made the individual the base of society — and of religion as well — and put individual responsibility above all forms of corporate responsibility or other social claims.

Its dictum is that people — individuals — should and do get pretty much what they deserve in all things, whether success on earth or later entry into heaven.

This is a view that much of the modern world regards as reactionary, while Texans themselves like to see it as futuristic, the hoped-for shape of things to come.

Meanwhile, it is a source of tension, not only between Texans and Northern "liberals" (many Texans are liberal, so long as liberalism does not touch religion, private property, the family, or openly enhance the powers of the state), but within the Anglo-Texan soul itself. For in the modern world of Texas as in all worlds there is a struggle between culture and practicality, dreams and reality, symbolism and structure, myth and truth, in short, a conflict with many names but which might be called, man wrestling with himself.

The old society is gone, but its imagery, mentality, and mythology live on. These are as alive in boardrooms across Texas as among the oil derricks and on the cattle ranges. The residue still shows in a hard pragmatism and absence of ideology, a worship of action and accomplishment, a disdain for weakness or incompetence, and a thread of belligerence – and finally, a cultural mythology stemming from the Alamo that even a Texan in the White House could not shake off.

Cultural survival is perhaps strongest in the ideal of the independent Texan. Now, this is not a purely Texan trait; it is American, found as much in the stony soil of New Hampshire as on the flinty plateaus of the Texas Hill Country. But the myth and cultural reality of personal independence is peculiarly and historically prevalent west of the Sabine and south of the Red River. The term "independent Ohioan" or "independent New Yorker" is essentially meaningless; if anything it conjures up images of political ticket-splitters. "Independent Texan," however, immediately strikes a chord of response among Texans, and even among other Americans who could not hope to define it.

The reality exists, from an H. L. Hunt to a Don Meredith to a Howard Hughes to a Bill Clements. Whether Texans damn such persons or praise them, they all evoke a haunting uneasiness and sense of loss that we associate with endangered species. For the person who demands independence and assumes personal responsibility – but not responsibility for others – has taken on the aspect of a vanishing tribe in modern America.

There were never so many "independent" Texans as folklore insists, just enough to fashion that folklore and impress it upon the Texan consciousness. There were the tall men who died at the Alamo and won at San Jacinto, all the while taking orders with poor grace. There were Rangers who rode alone like paladins; cattlemen who held their ranges against writs and wire as stubbornly as any feudal baron confronted with the king's cannon. There were the farmers who took their families into the Post Oak belt when it was still Comanche country and lived, by choice, miles from every neighbor. There were statesmen like Sam Houston who saved the nation one day and dared and damned the popular fury the next — heroes in heroic times, who stood for many different things, but created a rich Texas symbolism.

Like the society itself, the Texan hero was both futuristic and reactionary, in the vanguard but also representing something very old, seizing upon the latest techniques in the pursuit of primordial drives and goals.

Both old-coot cattlemen and early wildcatters fit the image, together with modern entrepreneurs. And this image has another dimension in Texas — that of men and women who jeer at the pretensions and hypocrisies of overly organized societies, whether they be European or Yankee or even those closer to home. It is the image of a Texan who speaks his mind in pungent, barnyard terms, and who can outwit, ignore, or overcome the absurdities and humiliations forced on most people by civilization.

This hero can just as easily be a cowboy as a range king, a jackleg as well as a millionaire tycoon. Texas is the last home of the jackleg (the person who would never join a labor union, a trade association, or a cooperative) as much as it is the refuge of the entrepreneur. The hero can be rightwing or radical, football player or country sheriff, or horse doctor — the view and style are not so important as is the ability to be one's own man and make it stick.

It helps, but is not necessary, for the hero to be a "good ole boy" in the Southern tradition.

To those with a sense of social organism this Texan is distasteful and even dangerous. But the ethos is not truly anti-social. The Texas hero is not set against society as such so long as society lets him be. Nor is this Texan a revolutionary in the modern sense. He is a rebel but has no interest in building a brave new world or reforming society; he rebels, like the rebels of 1836, to secure his own freedoms *within* society.

The independent Texan rarely is interested in pushing his own ideas or biases on others, so long as others do not try to make him abide by theirs. Then, there is a thin line between belligerence and aggressive self-defense, and because of this, an aura of violence always surrounds the Texan folk ideal.

If Texans often seem to be "agin" something or somebody, it is because independence is not a normal civilized human condition. Man is a social animal, seemingly as hierarchical as baboons (but not so successful at making hierarchies). Independence, the assertion of the individual under self-control, is only achieved with strain, preserved only by isolation or combat. The Texan ideal is the antithesis of the dropout – but also the antithesis of the organization man. It suggests constant, dubious battle.

Over most of the United States "independence" has a fine sound; it cannot be given a perjorative meaning in the American tongue, but it is something celebrated on July Fourth and forgotten the rest of the year. It is a wishful ideal, perhaps the last heritage of the old frontier.

Most Americans do not think independently or act independently, whether voting, buying, dressing, investing, or holding forth in intellectual circles. The independent person is praised but not often tolerated, a wonderful American kind of hypocrisy.

Financial independence rather than riches is probably the most prized American goal, which Merrill Lynch, land developers, and the Social Security planners all exploit expertly. Millions of Americans profess political independence, forcing countless politicians to portray themselves as "independent" Democrats or Republicans. The word still has magic in a vast, impersonal socio-economic-political system which in fact has made most forms of independence increasingly unobtainable.

But it is still this unsurrendered ideal that keeps some people slaving eighteen hours a day at personal enterprises when they could make more money on someone's payroll. It drives women professionals as well as would-be entrepreneurs. It drives a few from the rat race, but it hounds far more to the smogs of Denver or Houston, because Texas, like most of America, has developed irreconcilable imperatives.

The Frenchman Raymond Aron, perhaps the best observer of the American scene since Tocqueville, wrote that since the democratic revolutions of the eighteenth century, Western civilization has fostered strong, splendid ideals of personal freedom but at the same time created industrial, economic, and social forms which limit genuine liberty for the individual and family.

But capitalism is hardly the villain; the fault lies in any society driven to mass production, mass employment, mass consumption, and mass social organization. Under either a modern "capitalist" or "socialist" system, the roles, education, status, and psychological problems of clerks, sanitation workers, factory hands, educators, and engineers are much the same.

The clash between imperatives is also not new. The Texas-Mexican, Texas-Indian wars were cultural confrontations with racial overtones — but the struggle for the land was and is a war of cultural imperatives. The Indian ranges were appropriated by conquerors who were themselves conquered by an all-engulfiing civilization.

All these successive battles for cultural survival left their mark on the land, and on both the Texan and American soul. They form, at bottom, the stuff of Western literature, that most American of art forms, in which some lonely soul, perhaps aided by family and a friend or two, is always arrayed against vast odds at High Noon.

Those who find the Texan character uncomfortable or distasteful — including some Texans — disparage this image of the Texan hero, mock the myth of the man who stands alone, criticize the constant chimera of the Alamo. No matter —

every successive generation of Texans seeks its Alamos, and sometimes finds them.

The society of the Republic of Texas was remarkably simple, a rawer Old South writ large. It continued the traditions and tensions of Cohee and Tuckahoe between the upland corn farmers and the cotton-growing coastal plains. It was comprised of a horde of subsistence farmers and a smaller number of planter capitalists whose major investment was in Negro slaves. But rich man and poor man were racially, culturally, and religiously homogeneous — for all that the planters tended to be Anglican or Presbyterian and the others, (formally unchurched) puritan fundamentalist — in a characteristically American fashion. The rich man's life style was light years removed from the poor man's in many ways, but it was only what the poor man would have chosen, if he had had the means. There were few intimations of aristocracy, for aristocracy on the European pattern was despised. The planters were capitalistic rather than paternalistic in their world view, and the nearest insinuation of aristocratic notions was a reference to origins in Virginia or South Carolina. Such ancestry was considered — and to some, still is — more prestigious than that from other states.

Out of this odd mix was forged a genuine white democracy in which social and political equality, but never economic equality, prevailed. The cement was not so much class as the racism a black-owning society must have. The slaves provided a social floor.

The "respectable" occupations had already been established: landowner, farmer, doctor, lawyer. Texas was overrun with members of this last category from the earliest days. Anglo-Texans almost never engaged in merchandising or banking. The first practitioners of these trades came from the North — Presbyterian merchants who came down the Ohio and Mississippi Valleys — or directly out of Europe. Northern businessmen, like Richard King and Mifflin Kenedy and others less well-known from New England or New York, tended to become landowners and even slaveholders quite rapidly. This left commerce almost entirely to German or German-Jewish immigrants, and it was they who established almost all the stores and businesses across Texas from the Red River to the Rio Grande.

The Civil War desolated and demoralized this society but did not essentially change it across the eastern half of the state. Its basic human and cultural patterns were in fact reinforced by wholesale immigration of whites from the more devastated regions of the South, most of whom headed toward the frontiers.

By 1865, however, there was a very high proportion of blacks in Texas, partially because slavery was profitable here before the war, and partially because during the federal invasions of nearby states such as Louisiana and Arkansas, thousands of blacks had been sent by their owners to the relative safety west of the Sabine. What to do with this people — more than twenty percent of the population — and with the increasing numbers of poor whites ruined by the economic conditions that punished small farmers during the rest of the century after emancipation, could have become an insoluble problem without the institution of share-cropping.

This was a form of tenantry that did not involve cash payments, in which land was parceled out in small acreages to both white and ex-slave families. The landowner financed seed and other expenses, sometimes groceries, and after "deducts" took at least 20 percent of the value of the harvest. Reduced to his labor, the sharecropper found it almost impossible to rise from poverty. The system was not so pernicious as slavery or the debt-peonage that prevailed in Mexico, where debts legally bound the workers to the soil. It was even necessary in its time and place, if the population was to work and the land be used at all. But the effects on large parts of Texas society were profound.

It maintained the two-tier system of owners and workers — and as thousands of white families were driven into tenantry by the economic crises of the last part of the century, it created a newer class of "white trash." These were people of little ambition and slovenly habit, whose children, fed on a staple of syrup and cornbread, developed pellagra and worse, what in Texas came to be called the sharecropper mentality. The deprivations, real and cultural, of tenantry were harder to erase than the physical effects when country people moved to town in this century. Lyndon Johnson's grandfather was a community-founding pioneer, but his father was reduced to tenantry, and the President never quite escaped from or shook off the incubus.

Meanwhile, the ethnic Mexican population in Texas remained very small. It was no more than 12,000 (out of more than 600,000) before the Civil War, and was confined to the border regions south of San Antonio. In the towns and counties along the Rio Grande, political control passed entirely to Anglos, while the tenor of Mexican life remained unchanged. Texas Mexicans were rarely sharecroppers in this era. They were landowners themselves — as oppressed as the Anglo small farmers and gradually losing their lands — or laborers; they also made up a great proportion of the cowboys on Texas ranches in the Southwest.

Before 1900 there was almost no Mexican immigration, simply because there was nothing to attract it to the state. In 1900, ethnic Mexicans, who lived mostly in the borderlands, made up only five percent of all Texans, and they were almost ignored in the consciousness of the rest of the population — which was also to have its effects.

The rural character of Texas persisted very late. In 1860 the largest town, San Antonio, held only 8,000 citizens, and there were only twenty communities in all that boasted 1,000 inhabitants. In 1875, Washington County on the Brazos River was the most populous in Texas, and it did not contain a single town.

However, the movement from the land had already begun. This was to come in a steady tide, with repeated waves in the bad times of recurrent drouth and economic depression. But as late as 1910 there was no city with 100,000, and San Antonio, then as now without significant industry, was the largest in the state — a rank it was to hold until the 1930s when Houston, with its new man-made port, expanded under the impetus of the East Texas oil fields.

The trend toward urbanization accelerated throughout the twentieth century, with two-thirds of all Texas counties steadily losing population, while the Texas population itself grew prodigiously. However, as late as 1940 Texas was still predominantly rural, a fact that is not always understood outside the state.

The Texas cities, with a few exceptions such as Galveston and San Antonio, are all essentially twentieth-century creations. They all grew basically as mercantile, distribution, or financial centers for the countryside, or as ports of entry. And until well past the middle of this century, they were peopled primarily from the surrounding rural areas, from Old American agrarian stock. In most cases, they became metropolitan areas, some fifty in all, without the development of manufacturing industry.

Here there was a great difference from the patterns of the North and Midwest, where cities swelled from direct immigration from Europe, by populations that bypassed the trans-Appalachian experience, and most quickly developed industries.

Texas cities also grew up in the automobile age and were founded in almost every case in prairie or open country, unhindered by older surrounding settlements. Thus they expanded laterally rather than upward, without internal compression or close patterns forced by transportation needs. Few if any row houses were ever built in Texas; few if any neighborhoods — except for black and later Mexican enclaves — were ever formed.

Houston drew from the piney woods and surrounding rice plains; Dallas from the cotton belt; San Antonio from the limestone hills and dusty *brasada* country; four-score lesser cities did the same. Most Texans, moving from country to town, moved less than 200 miles — and this was not so much like Scotsmen going to London or Poles to Chicago but more like Frenchmen moving from their villages to neighboring Lyons.

City dwellers took up new occupations, but culture and world views did not immediately change. Farmers who saw themselves as middle class became white-collar employees — however, they did not, and still have not, become urbanites in cities with old, established urbane traditions.

During most of this century there was no fundamental change. Despite the profound depopulation of the rural counties, strong ties with them remained. Texans living in the burgeoning cities retained much of their rural outlook and ethos, along with their fried foods and small-town gaucheries.

Significantly, while each Texas city took on a certain ambience and character of its own — Dallas, earnest, eager, on the make; Houston, with its eye on the big buck; San Antonio and El Paso, less ambitious, more laid back and with virtually closed social circles at the top — none of them developed a true civic culture or civic type, like Parisians or Londoners or the natives of Hamburg. Texas culture, not civic culture, dominates. When a Texan is asked his place of origin, the native will almost always say "Texas," never "Houston" or "Amarillo." Sub-identifications come later, like the exchange of religious denomination or occupation.

The Texans also kept their Christian culture virtually unchanged. Texas is not a more merciful or more deeply religious society than others, but it is a *Christian* society. Religious forms permeate society and culture, from grace-saying to the public invocations by preachers — which some outlanders find uncomfortable or even distasteful — at football games. The churches are large, filled, and whatever effect they have upon faith and morals, they are an important means of Texan self-identification. Denomination is often as important as ancestry or occupation in defining identity, and each plays its role in society in a way that is unfathomable to many Americans to whom religion is no longer of significance.

If Texas had an established church — though the very notion goes against the grain of frontier American tradition — it would undoubtedly have emerged as Southern Baptist. For many years Baptists formed an absolute majority in the state, and their influence is still pervasive. Baptists evolved more powerfully in Texas than perhaps in any other region, and they have exported themselves more successfully than any other denomination into other American regions. Baptist polity fits Texas, both molding and reinforcing its world views: the essential priesthood of all believers, the lack of tension between God and Mammon and the acceptance of worldly success from effort, the separation of different ethnic groups as natural (which Catholics and mainstream Protestants handle uncomfortably), the puritan ethic with its distaste for pretension and luxury, belief in personal sin and personal salvation with the individual at the center of the religious universe, and suspicion of alcohol, disinterest in formal credos, and the utter independence of each congregation with disdain of elaborate hierarchies and rituals.

Besides the Baptists, many other pentecostal churches abound, both in the big cities and the rural areas.

Their influence in and on the culture has often been obscured, because other presences have been more visible. The early church buildings in Texas towns were all built by Episcopalians, Presbyterians, and Roman Catholics — who perhaps had greater need for edifices. In fact, until well into this century, Baptists and Methodists in Texas rarely erected buildings, and the first ones look more like courthouses than churches. As in most other parts of America, the socially elite — but not necessarily all rich people — gravitate toward more genteel denominations, and they draw more attention and make more news than the thousands of individual fundamentalist congregations who more often than not live in a state of truce with each other.

However, all the Texas churches — like all trans-Appalachian Protestants and even Roman Catholics assimilated into Anglo culture — are suffused with certain Calvinistic or puritan cultural values having nothing to do with their formal theology. On most issues, Anglicans and Baptists in Texas in the same community think, act, and vote much the same, leaving their disdains and quarrels, except for a few things like drinking, to distant theologians.

Texans also carried their basic social and economic forms from the countryside into the cities. While it is too simplistic to say the underclass is still black or brown and the rest of society is divided between owners and hired hands, something of this pattern clearly remains.

But since urbanization took place without the large-scale industrialization that was normal in the North, and was carried out by a different type of population, the forms and attitudes of American Northern industrial society have been slow to appear in Texas. In fact, they probably never will appear in exactly the same form. Here there is a very real difference between the society of Texas and the other "imperial" states. Texas did not create a new American urban culture out of many diverse parts; it adapted the rural frontier culture to an urban environment — but again, a different type of urban setting.

While urban Texas grew rich from the effects of extracting, processing, financing, and selling the state's products — and servicing all the processes — it was difficult for a real management structure to arise. Owners continued to profit most, but without the employment of large, blue-collared work forces, there was also nothing like the Eastern millowner-millhand relationship. Because most enterprise stayed small, there was no formation of private business into private bureaucracies in the classic American pattern.

The property owner has remained boss. All managers, from

ranch foremen to employed corporate executives to symphony conductors, hold at least something of the status of hired hands. And few things cause more misunderstaindings, confusion, and sometimes fury, among the newcomers who have entered Texas.

This pattern permitted Texas business to remain small and entrepreneurial, and it kept its ethic pure — but the side effects puzzle and even infuriate skilled people from other regions, whether music directors in Dallas who believe themselves above patrons' beck and call, or executives — but not owners — who see themselves as movers and shakers in some cities but are not invited into the most prestigious local businessmens' clubs.

In most Texas communities, certainly in the medium-sized cities and until very recently in such larger cities as Houston and San Antonio, economic, social, and political power have not fragmented as they have in the complex, ethnically mixed North. These have stayed in the same hands, a manifestation that Texas society remains more like American society of the last century than the present one. The society of Texas towns, like the basic Texas property laws, resembles that of America everywhere in the eighteenth century more than that of modern Boston.

This society has enormous disparities of wealth and divisions between the social classes — but these gulfs still tend to be obscured, or even unadmitted, because of the white population's essential homogeneity.

And this has the effect of enforcing a certain egalitarianism in what is not an egalitarian society, even within a rural Baptist congregation. Texans are awkward about expressing notions of birth or breeding, except as applied to those outside the Anglo race and culture. Ancestry is often traced to the older Southern states, with the inference that it was there high-up on the social scale — unprovable and immaterial in any case. Rich Texans, especially those descended from the old breed, manifest their wealth in certain visible symbols, but the automobile, great house, and private airplane are much more "right" in feel and practice than assertions of superior culture, whether of education, musical awareness, or the collection of antiques. Above all, wealth and power are most properly displayed in one's business, by buying a company, a vast ranch, prime breeding stock, or a bank.

Some of this, like the wearing of diamond jewelry by men, is mere gaucherie by the standards of old money, but some of it still comes from deep cultural springs. Many prominent Texans have their clothing custom-made, but still styled to make them look like cowboys.

As a major figure in the petroleum industry once said — both belligerently and defensively — compared to Eastern investment types most Texas oil men live like slobs, and would be made nervous by having a butler around the house.

Texas money is mostly new, though there is more "old money" around than even many Texans realize, but it has not taken all the courses followed by the mainstream. Just as some Scottish lairds still survive in stone castles on a damp rock surrounded by their gillies and pipers, some Texans who prepared with Greek for Harvard wear khakis and drive pickup trucks and surround themselves, not with baronial splendor, but with "Mexican" hired hands.

But beneath the ranks of owners and the handfuls of high executives, what was once an American middle class — bankers, merchants, professional people — tends more and more to become a New Class of salaried hands, privileged compared to those who perform manual labor, but hired hands all the same. They find the same fragmentation, in Texas, between emotion and intellect in their work, which often is not directly productive and in which they are judged less by results than by the approval of superiors and peers.

No part of life, from the university to the highway department, has excaped the pressures of modern organization and bureaucratization. The old discipline of self-reliance, still held, struggles with the newer social discipline of conformity.

National norms and fashions batter continually at the Texas frontiers, and the barriers do not always hold.

But there is still an instinctive clinging to a sense of time and place and uniqueness, however damaged by the national insistence upon total pluralism. As Joe Frantz, the Texas historian has observed, Texans find themselves somewhat in the position of eighteenth-century Scots confronting union with England. They treasure their differences, their social ethic and independence and society suffused with the forms, practices, and imagery of puritan Christianity, but at the same time are aware that others despise these and deprecate those who cling to them. The Texan who hopes to succeed in all senses of the word is torn between imperatives.

There is still a deep attachment to the land and its history, and pride in the way it all turned out, a pride lost in the ephemeral present of most American cities. This is what Texans mean when they say they are proud to be Texans, to newcomers who have shown their own pride and attachment to the places of their birth by their alacrity to leave them forever for a few more dollars.

Many Americans see these Texan traits as provincialism. And so they are, for Texans are provincial in most meanings of the word. But provincialism has always placed more strain on native intellectuals — born to a country where intelligence, but not intellectuality, is prized — than upon citizens who do what comes naturally, whether they be workers or businessmen. Texas intellectuals face the provincial's eternal dilemma: to go or not to go to Rome, and when in Rome, to try to become a Roman or make his living explaining his barbrian ways to Romans — who may find them greatly entertaining. It is a problem every Texas writer and artist faces in his own way. Some, like Scots or Gascons, make their way to London or Paris — but few ever really feel comfortable with the choice unless they can easily repudiate their heritage.

Modern American liberalism, for example, has its ironies: it asserts the right of Nigerians and Vietnamese to be Nigerians and Vietnamese — even when removed to America — but casts deep suspicions on the Texan who insists upon being a Texan.

This accounts for an agonizing confusion, both in and outside of Texas, about what Texas is and stands for and means to the greater nation.

It accounts for the self-exiled Texan, making a big to-do about it all in alien places, and for the agony of the Texas politician with ambitions beyond the state — who knows that he cannot placate both Dallas and New York, and that what may be conventional wisdom in one is likely to be anathema in the other.

And it also accounts for that ever-recurring phenomenon, the returning prodigal, come home at last.

CHAPTER VI

THE POLITICS

POLITICS and government — unless imposed by force or forces beyond local control — always arise from society, never shape it.

Foreign observers, whether European or Asian, often perceive this fact about Texas more clearly than some Americans. If they study the history of Texas — an emerging frontier peopled predominantly by puritan Protestants from the South and border states; if they view the economy — a vast agrarian-mining complex that is essentially colonial in its relationship vis-à-vis the United States and the world; and if they understand the nature of the society — white, middle-class, and dominated by property holders but not necessarily the larger ones — they tend to grasp the patterns and realities better than those natives who naively expect the same ideals and practices to prevail from coast to coast, simply because Texas is a state of the Union.

Texas politics and government emerged from Texas society, its ethos, imperatives, and world views, but is also hammered constantly by blows and pressures from outside, namely from the federal government. In these battles Texans have both won and lost. They have generally taken their humiliations by the nation with good grace — however, many changes, reforms, and laws that have brought Texas closer to the national norm would never have come about without the constant pressure of the federal Congress and courts. And the consciousness of this is always somewhere in the Texan heart and mind.

Since politics arise out of society, in the politics of Texas one finds what one would expect: a democracy with politics of the right, suffused with a property-holder's ethos, friendly to the concept of private right.

One finds the historic and continuing infusion of moral issues, such as alcohol and gambling, into politics.

One finds a powerful fiscal conservatism among the voters, if not always among the officials.

One finds a majority of citizens sharing the same basic political views, regardless of faction or party, in which there is a strong aversion to regulation and taxes, and to governmental power itself.

One finds no tolerance of criminality, above all of crimes against property, and a legal system in which conviction for armed robbery frequently draws heavier penalties than for mayhem or murder.

One finds little interest in political theory or ideology, much emphasis upon practicality — a true politics of the art of the possible, a politics of what is, not what might be.

One finds historic, continuing resistance to the mandating of national norms by the federal courts and Congress upon the provincial society.

Finally, despite all the color, foofaraw, and the regularly and nationally watched fireworks of Texas politics, there is not a great interest in politics itself. Government is supposed to do its job, which is to defend life, property, and basic liberties, and the majority of respectable and responsible citizens do not really care who governs Texas so long as it is governed in these interests.

On the surface, Texas politics has usually appeared to be

dominated by personalities, one flamboyant character accusing another, as in the days of the Republic when the heroes of San Jacinto, Sam Houston and Mirabeau B. Lamar, vied for the presidency, each accusing the other of being the biggest liar, drunkard, and public thief. Under the surface, however, there are usually real issues, as between Houston's Peace Party and Lamar's War Party. While apparent class divisions and interests are subdued, the voting public is usually aware of the more "conservative" or more "liberal" candidates and can make its choices accordingly. There are, of course, regional interests and constituencies.

Texans have often admired, rarely loved, their political heroes from Sam Houston to Lyndon Johnson. They have also despised them. In almost all cases, they have never really trusted them. This must be understood to understand Texas politics: the majority of Anglo-Texans have always seen and still see themselves threatened by elected spendthrifts who try to dazzle the people while selling out to the "interests" and dipping into their constituents' pockets.

Aside from this, politics in Texas is regarded as great fun by players and spectators alike. Rarely, if ever, do the lives, property, or wives of the citizenry appear in danger, despite the old saw, while the legislature is in session. Politics is not all that important to the average citizen who is not regulated or seeking favors from local government. And as everywhere else in the United States, politics is largely financed by those parties who seek favors or are regulated, such as developers and utilities.

Texans have tried, successfully, to put severe limits on political power, above all in the ways it may affect private property or change society. The majority of Texans have always perceived their true enemy: forms of power arising from any association other than a taxpayers' league.

Politics and government are seen by many Texans in the old American way — as necessary evils. Most Texas politicians sense this (and some share the view) and act accordingly. This is the great despair of liberal Texans – and there is a vocal liberal minority – but they pick the wrong target when they attack officeholders. The real problem for those with a variant view of government is society itself.

A favorite saying of the Texas frontier was "Root, hog, or die." It arose among the settlers who turned their swine out to forage for themselves, as later they did with cattle. It was not a quaint or folksy phrase, as some see it today; it had a basis in hard reality. And it showed a frontier-pragmatic frame of mind that applied to more than hogs, and which has never really disappeared among the dog-run dwellers' white-collared descendants.

The people who entered Texas were expected to root; they set their own goals and carried them out in their own way. This has been called "rugged individualism," but at the bottom it was a "God helps those who help themselves" philosophy, and it was expressed in Anglo attitudes toward government.

Some of the early Texas colonists came to Texas to escape government; in any case, they were all descended from people who had rebelled against the British Crown and despised Americans who tried to rule over them. Nothing more showed their unconcern with the American nation and state than their willingness to migrate beyond the Sabine into foreign territory.

The settlers, especially the more successful, had no quarrel with Mexican sovereignty – until centrist regimes in Mexico began to assert government upon them. Even then, the larger farmers were exceedingly reluctant rebels. The agitators of the Texas Revolution were largely late-comers, lawyers, and adventurers with a small stake in Mexican Texas, trusting in an overthrow to make things better. Only when it became apparent that the Mexican dictator would not reason with them – and when Stephen F. Austin, who went to Mexico, was thrown in jail – did the planters rally to the call to arms.

After the establishment of the Texan nation, this same dichotomy between the stable, propertied men and the restless frontier continued. The Republic had plenty of land and it was consciously founded as a Jeffersonian democracy in which every male family head was entitled to land, was expected to work it, and defend his rights on it — and in fact, as a residue of Spanish law, the property rights of married women were also guaranteed.

Both coastal planters and upland corn farmers wanted and made a state that did not and could not plan society — they saw this as an immoral intrusion upon personal liberty — and in fact had almost no control over society in general. Texans were not an anarchic people, but they were a difficult people to rule.

The Republic's Constitution reflected a landowner's bias. It kept government localized and weak, basically organized in counties. It provided a three-year term for a popularly elected president who could not succeed himself. No clergyman could serve in the legislature, assuring separation of church and state — in which the people strongly believed. Private homesteads were exempted from foreclosure, and there were restrictions upon all private corporations and banks — in fact, it was impossible to form a private corporation or bank.

Direct taxation of the people was considered unthinkable, and the Republic's revenues were restricted to fees and customs duties.

The basic aims and biases of this constitution governed all successive state constitutions, from 1845 to 1876.

However, cohesion was more apparent than real. Limitless land and the root-hog philosophy did not mean that all hogs could find sustenance, and the frontier families along the southern and western borders needed defense against Mexican and Indian incursions. They demanded protection without any means to pay for it, while the eastern counties, secure and more concerned with stable government and sound credit, preferred that the westerners root for themselves.

The tensions quickly entered politics. President Sam Houston, the hero of San Jacinto, emerged as leader of the planter class, seeking peace with the Mexicans and Indians, trying to establish a sound financial system. He could do none of these things successfully, and his successor, Mirabeau B. Lamar, was swept in by the swelling frontier vote.

Lamar was the rootless, restless, land-hungry frontier's darling. He shared its hatred of all Indians, asserting that the white and red races could not share the same continent. He also possessed the frontier's essential belligerence. He was a nationalist with no interest in joining the United States. He dreamed of expanding Texas to the Pacific. When the Mexicans refused to make peace, he made war — so far as Texas was able — and he was determined to destroy the Indians.

Whatever the justice of Lamar's actions, they were historically successful. The eastern tribes, mainly semi-civilized agrarians like the Cherokees, were swept up and driven out of East Texas, opening up the whole region to white settlement. Punitive expeditions broke the power of the Southern Comanches, though not the long-ranging Northern bands, and brought uneasy peace to the southern frontier. His expeditions to Santa Fe and south of the Rio Grande proved to be utter fiascos; but meanwhile the little Texas Navy under Commodore Moore raised havoc with Mexican shipping on the Gulf and also supported Mexican rebels in Yucatan.

By acting like a proper nineteenth-century nation, Lamar's Texas won diplomatic recognition from France and Britain — and convinced men in the United States, where the possible annexation of Texas was halted by fears of war with Mexico and the opposition to any extension of slavery, that Texas meant business.

But these activities were expensive for a nation of twenty-three rural counties. The Indian campaigns cost millions; the navy was extremely costly. Since Texas had no credit or ability to borrow, the government issued paper money, the "red back" notes which immediately fell to a dime on the dollar.

The glory that was Texas began to founder in financial chaos.

This brought Houston back in a landowners' *revanche* with a new, planter-dominated Texas Congress. Now, the Peace Party began to run Texas government like a retail store, much to the War Party's (and probably all Texas politicians') disgust: dozens of offices were abolished, salaries were reduced to honoraria, the army was replaced with a few Ranger companies, the navy was ordered sold — although the citizenry of Galveston, who had by then fallen in love with the prospect of the Lone Star flag on the high seas, prevented this by armed action.

Houston, a protégé of Andrew Jackson, was an American, not a Texan, expansionist. His goal was always to bring Texas into the Union, while his political supporters never saw much future for Texas as a nation. Like the men who fashioned the U.S. Constitution in 1789, they distrusted powers and potentates and governments, but they desired a government strong enough to safeguard the frontiers without risking bankruptcy, defend the social order, and protect private property. The obvious solution was annexation. And it was strategic and financial considerations, rather than any call of "blood to blood" that motivated the majority.

Andrew Jackson's last official act had been to recognize the Republic of Texas, but from there the matter had been suspended. Lamar and the War Party, and for some years the majority of Texans on the frontier, showed no interest in pursuing it. Ironically, it was Lamar, not Houston, who opened the door to annexation. Men in the American government became concerned about the rise of a new, competing power on the continent, or even worse, a power allied with France or Great Britain, neither of which in that era had eschewed all American territorial ambitions. Northerners still hated the prospect of war with Mexico, and Abolitionists railed against any extension of the slave states, but they feared an independent Texas even more, so when Houston reopened the matter, Washington was almost frantic to conclude a treaty.

Houston and his Texans played their cards adroitly, continuing negotiations with France, Britain, and Mexico — the latter belatedly trying to acquiesce to de facto independence — even after the treaty was signed in 1844. In order to convince Texan political opinion to ratify the treaty, the United States sweetened the deal immensely, granting Texas concessions that no entering territory ever won before or afterward.

The U.S. recognized and agreed to defend Texas' claim to the Rio Grande boundary, although this included huge areas not under Texan control or settlement; to allow Texas to retain title to all public lands within these borders; and to assume all the Republic's debts, on terms favorable to Texas but costly to the Treasury. This proved a bonanza; the settlement for the cession of Texas' claims to New Mexican territory came to $10,000,000 — then an immense sum — even excluding the costs of the Mexican War which inevitably ensued. Manifest Destiny significantly lightened the U.S. Treasury.

Texans felt they had surrendered little but gained much, and as the Union was then construed, they had. The federal government now had responsibility for the frontiers, provided postal and other services, imposed a sound financial and credit system, but levied no direct taxes for any of this, while U.S. customs duties and imposts were actually lighter than the old Republic's. And the United States, under the prevailing concept of government, left all internal policy and regulation to the states.

Texans never intended to surrender as much sovereignty as they eventually did. This came about, not so much from the Civil War, but through changing concepts of national government in the twentieth century.

The aggressive, eternally hungry frontier was satisfied with the Rio Grande boundary and the retention of all Texas public lands by the state, for the state continued to give these away while the federal authorities then sold public lands for hard dollars.

Texas enacted a state constitution which faithfully copied the old one. The governor was elected for only two years; the legislature met biennially; high officials were at first appointed, but this was changed soon to popular election. Essentially the state government was given few powers; in fact, the governor was more a peer of county sheriffs than a chief executive. And all the old property-owners' biases remained: a two-thirds vote of the legislature was required to create any private corporation, and no bank could incorporate under any circumstances.

Significantly, quarrels between Austin and Washington arose at once.

Texans demanded that the federal government remove the remaining nuisance of the Indians in the west. Washington was reluctant. It was not, and would not be policy to destroy the western tribes as "independent" nations until Grant's second administration. The United States possessed no cavalry arm; the first mounted regiment was raised in 1856 for Texas border service by Secretary of War Jefferson Davis, but cavalry was expensive. Washington preferred to make treaties and try to bar whites from Indian territory – but in Texas this was impossible.

Since the U.S. owned none of the land the Comanches held – it was all state or private property under the law – the Indians were tenants-at-will, or trespassers. The government could not even grant them a reservation out of these territories, but for long years it hoped somehow to avoid conflict, while conflict continued and hundreds of frontier people died.

On the Texas frontier, impatience with and contempt for this policy were factors coloring the public's opinion toward Secession. In Indian policy and performance, Washington did not give Texans what they wanted and believed was their just due. Here some love was lost between state and nation.

In the events leading up to Secession in 1861, the patterns were similar to those of the revolt against Mexico. The frontier farmers owned no slaves; they hated the institution but also feared and despised blacks, free or slave. Yet the frontier, and the regions beyond the true black belt, were the most ardent for Secession. Again, lawyers were in the forefront of agitation. However, the large planters who owned almost all the slaves in Texas did not support outright rupture. They understood the colonial nature of the economy, and "sovereignty" meant little to them. They believed themselves better off under the protective umbrella of the United States.

While Lincoln, who threatened the institution of slavery, did not receive a recorded vote in Texas, the planters did not support the ardent states' rights candidate, Breckenridge, in 1860. They voted overwhelmingly for John Bell, the Conservative Union man, trying to uphold both the Union and slavery, which of course was constitutional at the time. These were the wealthiest, best-educated, and least parochially minded men in Texas, but Texas was not an aristocracy and the popular furor to secede prevailed, even over the stubborn opposition of Governor Sam Houston.

Although it became common to describe the War Between the States as a "rich man's war and a poor man's fight" when the South began to lose, in Texas this was never close to the truth. Once the war was inevitable, the planters exhausted their resources, shed their blood in higher proportion, and suffered the greatest losses.

While Union soldiers never penetrated Texas during the war — Texas' coastal defense was one of the superb feats of the Confederacy — the humiliation of defeat was just as complete in 1865. Ninety percent of the people had come out of the South; 90 percent supported the war; 90 percent believed the wrong side won. And the new Reconstruction government that was established by Federal occupation forces lacked the good will of 90 percent of all white Texans.

This Republican regime lasted only as long as it was backed by Federal bayonets, but the men involved were not all carpetbaggers and scalawags. They included honorable Texans and Northerners who in fact tried to make incisive reforms in the state. They centralized state government, established a state police, and founded a public school system. However, they also took part in the general corruption and favoritism toward corporations and railroads, and it was these latter activities that made a profound impression on the conquered Texans.

When the Republican Reconstruction administration was swept out in 1874, in a campaign redolent of fraud and violence on both sides, it was replaced by a Confederate government in almost every sense, filled with men who hated everything the Unionists had done. The Texans now proceeded to throw out the good with the bad, as alien, Yankee, and intolerable. The war and Reconstruction, the latter especially, created lasting animosities and mindsets, and they fashioned Texas into a one-party Democratic state for the foreseeable future.

The 1876 state constitution, much amended and tattered but still the fundamental law, was drawn up mainly by farmers and ranchers, and it embodied all their biases and ideals against the "interests," corporations, and centralized government. All the old forms were revived: frequently elected officials with small pay and little power, biennial sessions of the legislature, and harassment of railroads, banks, and corporations of all kinds. Only the state school system survived. Prior to Yankee occupation, Texas had never gotten around to creating one, and now too many citizens saw its merits.

The constitution was also very narrowly drawn, unlike the federal constitution. It specified not just what government might not do but also precisely what it could do, and no more. It arose out of a lasting distrust of government, a suspicion of government as potential tyranny, and it did not even give government the authority to create a water district without calling a special election to amend the constitution.

Naturally, in the course of human events such a constitution had to be amended many times, hundreds of times — but thus far, Texas voters have shown themselves extremely recalcitrant to alter its basic spirit. They have rejected continual efforts to replace it as decisively as they have blocked attempts to raise the pay of legislators or to allow the state government planning and spending powers in the vital area of water resources. The key has always been resistance to any extension of government power; amendments which do not threaten this pass relatively easily.

The governor, although his term eventually was raised to four years, has remained weak, less powerful in real terms than the lieutenant governor who controls the state senate in certain ways, or even the local county sheriff in the countryside. The salaries of state legislators are still essentially honoraria, and all except the legislators themselves are perfectly content with the arrangement.

The 1876 constitution played a significant role in the future of the state. In simplest terms, it went far to prevent Texas from becoming a major industrial state such as Michigan or Illinois. It hindered the growth of business corporations. Until the holding company device was found legal in very recent years, the ukase against branch banking stopped the growth of any major financial institution in the state. Farmers and landowners, not financiers, ruled: In Texas a homestead or a horse (later the law was extended to include the automobile) cannot be foreclosed for personal debt, and wages cannot be garnisheed. Texas became what Northern financial institutions shudderingly call a "debtor's state."

Here Texas politics and law tended to deviate from the national norm, with the result that a new front had been opened up, a defensive border against the North, creating an adversary situation similar to the Texans' old struggles against Mexico, Indians, and nature.

These attitudes were strengthened during the long agrarian crisis in which the century closed. The People's Party, or Populists, was born in Texas, at Lampasas in 1879. This was a political-action group of farmers, some large but mostly small and poor — "working men" as they called themselves — whose anguish and economic misery, as they were destroyed by economic trends, spilled furiously into local and national politics. Populist fury spread to other states in the South and Midwest, and for a time it actually shook the nation. The Populists frightened, although they never really threatened, American economic and financial organization, by railing at the "interests" they believed were the cause of their troubles: banks, railroads, corporations, gold, low prices, and tight credit. Sometimes they singled out the Jews, although most Populists had never actually seen one.

They demanded regulation and restriction of all the "interests" (meaning out-of-state corporations) and some of their demands were enacted, though with an ironic side effect. During the era when "outside" corporate business found it impossible to operate in Texas, local giants such as insurance and utility empires received a golden chance to emerge and grow.

However, most of the enemies of the Populists were distant chimeras, out of state and out of reach. And significantly, Populism never quite conquered the land of its birth. The basically conservative Democrats, though hard pressed, retained office in election after election — for this popular protest did not signify any sort of social or political revolution. Bankers in Boston might shake at the thought of sweaty farmers in overalls brandishing pitchforks, but Populist fury did not extend to the local merchant who carried poor men on credit, or to the genteel landowners who were suffering, albeit more comfortably than their less fortunate brethren.

At first, both poor white farmers and black tenants were united politically in this protest, but the color barrier turned out to be insurmountable. Despite most sincere and even desperate efforts by Populist leadership, white Populism soured into anti-Negro rancor, always latent, and the black man became as much the enemy as the "interests." Populist pressure as much as anything else led to the laws and devices that restricted black voting — poll taxes, registration — and in effect weakened the poor man's political protest.

Frustrated, Populism tended to diverge in two directions, namely racism and a drive for prohibition of alcholic beverages, which now dominated Texas politics, at least on the surface, for a generation.

The agrarian problem and agrarian protest were never assuaged by political action. They eventually died natural deaths: by 1900, farm prices were rising because of expanding markets in Europe and the rapidly growing cities in the North and East. The era between 1900 and 1914 was one of good times for farmers and ranchers; meanwhile, the less successful had left the land, moving on or gathering in Texas' own emerging cities.

The nature of Texas Populism is often misunderstood. It was in no sense Marxist or really revolutionary. The Populists wanted money in their jeans, not the overthrow of the social order — which was one reason they remained so hostile to Negro participation in politics. Texas Populists were against the forms of capitalistic organization that were rising in America, of which they saw themselves the victims. They had nothing against private — truly private — enterprise itself. Former populists had no quarrel with the basic scheme of things, and as soon as the times became bearable, there remained little or none of the idealism or social ideology that pervaded the Northern branches of the movement.

Populism passed; its rhetoric, along with a scattering of laws and enactments regulating Texas business, lingered. One ironic effect was that while Texas' anti-corporate laws kept most large national companies at bay, those same laws allowed the emergence of native insurance and utility companies that eventually became giants, powering the rise of Dallas and other cities. Another irony is that while the sons and grandsons of People's Party voters became business-oriented in the cities and found ways around the old laws to make Texas perhaps the state with the best "business climate" in the nation, the old imagery and rhetoric still persist. It is not safe for politicians to be "against business" or "anti-capitalist." It is perfectly acceptable, however, to be against the "interests."

After the rise and demise of Populism as a political force, certain patterns continued throughout the new century. The Democratic Party was the only respectable political organization, but it was not, and never became, a truly ideological or special interest political party like those which rose in Europe and in some states. Everybody in Texas (though there was always some submerged Republicanism among bankers, German-descended settlers, and immigrants out of the Midwest) was a Democrat, rich or poor, and therefore the Party had to be a vast umbrella, covering and serving all. It could not be ideological or special-interest oriented. It had to reflect the dominant views and interests of the people of the state.

These were, and remain, essentially conservative, socially, fiscally, politically, and philosophically, so far as philosophy exists.

This system had and has its faults — complacency and an amiable courthouse corruption is found in almost every corner of the state — but it has also served the state well. In a single-party state where political fights usually occurred only in the primaries — and then more often than not revolved around personalities and personal ambitions rather than real issues — the tendency was for Senators and Congressmen to become long-term incumbents. Texans rose in seniority in the Congress, gaining important leverage which allowed them to bring home many a Yankee dollar — an achievement against which even the most conservative rural Democrat had few if any scruples.

For long years Texas Democrats had no quarrel with their colleagues in the North and East; theirs was a purely political alliance. Democratic city bosses could run New York or Chicago as they chose so far as Texans were concerned, if they allowed Texas Democrats to run Texas the way the dominant majority wanted it. Texas, a solid part of the solid South, helped to elect Democratic Presidents and Democratic Congresses and shared in the spoils.

Like most of the South, Texas broke with the national party in 1928 over Al Smith's Roman Catholicism and open partisanship of alcohol. And while this made no significant change whatever in local politics, it showed a trend that would become more evident, over different issues, in later years. When the Northern Democrats diverged from the "good-ole-boy" arrangement and tried to impose alien notions on Texas voters, the "boys" in Texas would not go along.

Texans had no problems with the New Deal era. The Prohibition question, always vexing, was solved by the device of local option — an arrangement that as much as anything shows the Texan mind. If the people of a locality want liquor, they should have it, but if they don't, no one should have the power to mandate it on them. Franklin Roosevelt's New Deal, which generated even more mysticism and nonsense than the Populists, was not revolutionary. It eschewed social reforms; its main thrust was to put money in the people's pockets. This thrust, aided by Texas political power, was to pour a great deal of money into rural Texas with beneficial results.

However, an ominous split was apparent by 1944. Texas Democrats were infuriated by Roosevelt's choice of Wallace as his running mate. They saw Wallace as a dreamy-eyed, one-world liberal with whom they wanted no truck — and here began a dichotomy and division that quickly created two Democratic Parties in Texas.

The first, which remained dominant and was supported by the majority, was the conservative faction, believing in Yankee dollars but no Yankee dictation, and above all, no Yankee tinkering with society as God and the frontier had fashioned it.

The second faction, then and still in the minority, generally followed the line and lead of the national Party, which turned increasingly liberal and increasingly intrusive into business and society.

Each faction came to dislike the other almost as much as it hated the Republicans.

For a long time, in an era not completely ended, this gave the conservative Democrats something of the best of worlds. They could usually win the primaries, then call upon party unity in the general election against the Republicans. This normally worked well. Whipsawed, the liberals really had no choice.

The Eisenhower era, however, made Republicans respectable, if not loved, in Texas. Outraged by the image of Adlai Stevenson, the dominant faction among Texas Democrats supported Eisenhower both covertly and overtly, starting a precedent. Meanwhile, a small but growing Republican Party began to emerge in Texas cities. Its early leadership tended to be patrician, because only those with birth, breeding, and a deep purse, plus some suicidal instincts, found it comfortable on the Republican ticket, and its interests were less to elect Republican Presidents — like the old Republican patronage machine — than to establish a two-party state.

While the Republican impact on local elections was negligible in the 1960s, the Democrats in national elections were ceasing to carry a majority of the white vote.

Here again there was a difference from the North. There, the pattern was for the big cities to vote Democratic, the rural areas and small towns to cling to Republicanism. In Texas, this tended to be reversed. First, the ancient Confederate-Democratic loyalties were strong in rural East Texas. Second, because Texas cities were peopled differently from those in the North, the people had a different sort of politics. This was, or should have been, apparent when in 1948 Strom Thurmond, the Dixiecrat, carried Houston's Harris County, the largest metropolitan area in Texas. As in the case of Thurmond himself, the leap to Republicanism was not impossible under the proper pressures.

Republicans did not win Texas in 1972; the candidacy of George McGovern threw it away. This again was no more a watershed than the Hoover-Smith contest, but it showed the new structure of Texas politics.

Few Texans loved Nixon, but most detested everything the cold-eyed, social-reforming McGovern seemed to stand for. Here lines seemed clearly drawn, and the liberal Democratic vote statewide was reduced to its hardrock bottom, about one third of the electorate. So far as analysis can determine, this vote was largely comprised of black and Hispanic minorities, trade unionists, and a sprinkling of academics and intellectuals. The white middle class voters were "turned off" almost completely.

The candidacy of the Southerner Jimmy Carter in 1976 confused the issue sufficiently so that East Texas swung the balance, making Texas the only major state west of the Mississippi that Carter carried.

In 1978, the election of William P. Clements, Jr., the first Republican governor since Reconstruction, surprised most observers. It did not, however, signify the emergence of a true two-party state, because again the best analysis showed that no more than a third of all Texans had formed any lasting attachment to the Republican Party. Two thirds of all Texans may be political conservatives, but two thirds are also Democrats.

The Reagan-Carter shootout in 1980 merely confirmed the Nixon-McGovern pattern. The issue was not party, but the public's perception of liberal-conservative, pro-government-anti-government delineations.

Politics in Texas does not break down exactly into philosophy, social class, economic interest, or regionalism any more than elsewhere in the United States. Personalities, mood, local issues can be ephemerally important. Flaming liberals have been, and can be elected both in enclaves and statewide. But when the issue is clearcut between a fiscal and social conservative and someone straying from these principles, the liberal vote rarely exceeds 40 percent and is often smaller.

In most current politics the issue is not always raised, although candidates try to make points of being "more" liberal or conservative than the others. Liberals with good sense almost never attack private enterprise or property or advocate directly the spending of money. The preferred tactic is to attack the "interests" and suggest that they have undue influence, both with government and the opposing candidate. Populist rhetoric, meaningless in practice, is very fashionable.

The emergence of the minority vote, blacks in East Texas and the core cities, Hispanics in the south (and in fact, throughout Texas) has become crucially important. The conservative Democrats' dilemma is that the Party is failing to carry the white vote in many areas — but the political goals of the minorities, whose leadership generally wants government spending and social action on the behalf of minority citizens, are anathema to the dominant Democratic faction. The minority vote, when it can be isolated as in the Nixon-McGovern or Reagan-Carter elections, is not decisive. Statewide, it can rarely dominate more than enclaves. But as the white vote has become fragmented between Democrats and Republicans — with the emergence of a newer, much more ideological Republicanism in many parts of Texas — the votes of Hispanic Texans and blacks has become a deciding factor in many races. It is something to be wooed and won, though most Democrats and Republicans do not quite know how.

Meanwhile, the minority vote grows less monolithic and less "voted." It votes ethnically, just like the whites, but not always according to the dictates of leaders. The old, blatant racism of earlier years has virtually disappeared in politics; federal law, and the fact that no politico dares offend minority voters deliberately has ended it. Nor would the public mood support it, even among the more rabid conservatives. However, the black and brown minorities for all their growing voting strength, face the same fundamental problem of

Democratic mainstream liberals: the Anglo-Texan ethos which holds that people get what they deserve, and that voting themselves something they don't deserve is immoral.

However, the minority voters — as opposed to certain scattered groups — are clearly not radical in Texas. The "takeover" of dozens of south Texas communities by Hispanic elected officials, in a region where 90 percent of the population is Mexican-American, has resulted in no "brown dawn" or any revamping of society. Hispanic Texans, though with important cultural differences from Anglos, tend to be socially conservative, divided by class, and no more monolithic, in power, than the citizens of El Salvador. The Democrats have, in general, successfully co-opted the leadership, thus restraining and thwarting the purely ethnic political parties such as *Raza Unida*.

Black leadership, meanwhile, as exemplified by Barbara Jordan's behavior in the statehouse, has been even less radical. It pragmatically works with the power structures, and in fact, much mutual respect, if not love or friendship, has emerged in recent years between black and white political leaders.

The political pattern that has been perhaps most important in recent times, certainly adding to the growing Republican strength, is resistance to what the majority of Texans regard as continual interference by the national government in society and business and local government. This meets societal, philosophical, and sheer territorial opposition. The anger against mandating from Washington is subdued — after all, the issue of sovereignty has been settled — but profound, among both officials and the people.

Virtually no social or political change that has come about in Texas in the twentieth century has risen from public demand, or was voted by the citizenry. Whatever their merits, changes have been continually forced by courts or governments, in each case making Texas adopt national norms. The gamut runs from integration of the races to voting rights, from bilingual education to picketing laws, from districting to the 55-mile-per-hour speed limit, which most Texans resent and flaunt at will.

There is no real rebellion against these; no rebellion is possible. On some of the issues Texans are morally defensive, as with slavery in the last century. But just as they did not vote down slavery, they have not, and would not, have voted for the vast majority of government-induced reforms of Texas society. When the public or Texas officials can ignore federal mandates, they are disposed to do so; when they can fight them in the courts or in Congress, they do so with enthusiasm.

Moderate Democrats run on platforms pledging opposition to Washington "when it's wrong." The voters do not believe this will do any good — but it lets them know the candidate's heart is in the right place.

The fires are banked, not dead.

Texas politics and government have been much criticized, both within the state and out. The national image is not good. Unquestionably, both have their manifold failures and corruptions, but corruption is proportional, in most systems, to the amount of favors government can bestow or the pressure government regulation can exert. For this reason, Texas government may be less corrupt than that of many states, for the state government builds superb roads, polices the highways, taxes and regulates enterprise as little as possible; and does not take much else upon itself.

Public issues revolve more about who can get the most for the tax dollar than who can solve problems by spending more money.

Whoever the candidates or whatever the issues, a taxpayers' outlook and ethos predominates. Texas has not seen a taxpayers' revolt, a Proposition 13 as in California or Proposition 1½ as in Massachusetts because none has been necessary — the burdens have never been allowed to press that heavily on property owners. The fact that the state, from the oil bonanza, has run huge surpluses produces less satisfaction among the public than the politicians, for it is an indication that taxes may be too high — and the public is aware that politicians, even in Texas, can no more sit on surpluses than soldiers can sit on bayonets.

All this has produced, if not the best government in the world, a government that for the past 100 years has been clearly responsive to the wishes of the majority. It is also a state government whose methods and practices are now beginning to be studied by other states, for it works without continual fiscal crises.

Not only the state government but most Texas cities govern themselves essentially by *laissez-faire*. Houston is the largest city in the nation without a zoning code. The great majority of Texas cities elect councils comprised of local businessmen rather than professional politicians. The ceremonial mayor is preferred to one who is a strong executive; city councils are paid a pittance or not at all; and most are elected on a nonpartisan basis. The elected officials reign; the details are left to hired-hand professionals who are supposedly — but not always — removed from local politics. Nothing like the enormously expensive city and county governments in New York or most Northern states exists — the voting public simply will not put up with it.

If there is inevitably local slackness and inefficiency in public agencies, state offices tend to be slim, disciplined, and taut, even after an unprecedented growth during the 1970s. The state bureaucracy is too abused to be arrogant or abrasive. Those state and local services of which the majority approves, whether highways or agricultural extension services, range from excellent to splendid — those of which the public does not approve, in many cases do not exist at all.

Those agencies which have little esteem suffer accordingly in this democracy. Texas, especially in the 1980s, is relatively a rich state, and very rich in terms of revenues. It stands at the very bottom of the tier of poorest states, however, in the sums it expends for public health and welfare. Teachers' salaries always hover near the lowest in the nation, and if the majority is satisfied with this, there is a vocal minority that is not.

Whether Texas is dominated by the "interests" – the developers, utility companies, contractors, and various businesses that finance the majority of all American politics everywhere – or the people depends on how one defines "interests." The government certainly is not run by academics, labor leaders, or working men. But there is no evidence that it is run by the giant corporations or the fifty-seven Texans who are among the nation's 400 richest men, though it is run in a manner that they find acceptable and conducive to their prosperity.

Texas has no personal or corporate income tax, and there is no politician on the scene who is likely to propose one. Petroleum finances a third of all Texas public revenues, but the state gasoline tax in 1982 was the lowest in the nation.

The state brags about that. It does not brag about its social services, and it does not enjoy all the finger-pointing at the treatment afforded its minorities, poor, and elderly.

The frontiersman's grandson, in his Hathaway white collar and comfortable high-rise office, may no longer understand what "Root, hog or die" meant in the old days, but the essence of this harsh dictum continues to affect his world view.

CHAPTER VII

CHANGE

"CHANGE" is a sort of buzz word in American parlance, with vastly different meanings to different people. To some, the word conjures up an image of progress and opportunity; for others, it has a ring of insecurity, because nothing can be more unsettling. And for reformers of a certain stripe, "change" has become a euphemism for the abolition or disappearance of everything in society they dislike.

Texans over the years have learned that when outsiders, especially Northerners or liberals, investigate change in Texas, what they are really looking for is evidence that the state is becoming more like the other forty-nine.

On the surface, the evidence is overwhelming. Texans perform the same kinds of jobs, ride to work in the same kinds of cars, live in the same kinds of houses, and absorb the offerings of the same media as the rest of the country. Culturally, the major Texas cities do their best to copy Cleveland or Kansas City with symphony orchestras and professional sports teams, and the product is sometimes indistinguishable.

But the answer to the question "When is Texas going to become more like us?" is "Probably never."

This takes some perspective for many Americans to understand. Texas and the Texans are quintessentially American;

they are the culmination of a certain kind of American experience. Without the South and West, and the conquest of the South and West, American history is unthinkable. The nation would be as incomplete without Texas as it would be without the flowering of New England in the last century, or the emergence of the now-declining heavy-industry belt in the Midwest in this century. All these regions make up a vital whole, but it is a mistake to think they are, or should be, without significant differences. Such differences do emerge from demography and history and they are much slower to go away than many Americans want to believe.

Change is probably the most avidly studied topic in America, and it may be the least understood in one respect. This is, that while lands and peoples change continually under the various impacts of modern life, they do not normally change at the same pace, or in exactly the same way.

One of the great illusions of the modern world is that lands and peoples are growing more alike. This is believed even by those who fear it or don't want it to happen, such as the intellectuals of small nations who dread that they will be swallowed up in an amorphous worldmass. But simply because there is no difference anywhere in the world in the shape of machine guns or oil drums or in the principles behind their manufacture and use, this does not mean that a world which uses the same sort of weapons and energy sources is growing any closer in world view, or that its peoples are becoming indistinguishable. To believe in that kind of "One Worldism" is, perhaps, the ultimate American illusion, born of the melting-pot theory.

French influence was great in nineteenth-century Russia; however, the Russian is no more like a Frenchman today than he was before Napoleon's time. He may not be the *same* Russian, but he is a Russian all the same. A bureaucratic, despotic, xenophobic Czarist empire has turned into a bureaucratic, despotic, xenophobic Soviet empire — and from the perspective of historians some centuries from now, probably very little will seem changed.

Texas and Texans are changing and evolving, but they are not necessarily changing and evolving in the same way, or same directions, as all other Americans. They have not done so in the past, and there is very little in the present to suggest that they will do so in the future.

In fact, the rate and impact of change in recent years is much less than in the past. A Texan who lived from 1875 until 1950 experienced vastly more far-reaching changes in lifestyles than any American born within the past fifty or even twenty-five years. The Texan born on the Indian frontier or into a purely agrarian economy and ethos had to survive and surmount several shattering economic depressions and sea changes. He lived through the emergence of America into a world power. He had to adjust to the telephone and telegraph, the radio and television, the automobile and aircraft, and the much more jarring shift from countryside to city and town.

Americans born since the turn of the century have only had to cope with refinements of a scientific society already in motion, one that is markedly still drawing upon the capital of earlier decades.

It would seem that Texas society, having survived the shocks of the past hundred years while retaining so much of its invisible ethos and so many of its visible societal patterns, could easily survive another century as long as the fundamentals of the land do not change.

It is always difficult to distinguish between cosmetic changes and genuine transformations of character. A person in a custom-made shirt and a hand-tailored suit may retain both a barbarian hardihood and a primordial worldview for a very long time.

Tocqueville's study of Americans easily fitted Anglo-Texans of his time. But Tocqueville reads very well today, not only as applied to Texas but to much of the United States. There is much more continuity to society and culture despite dilutions and surface changes than most Americans like to admit. Tocqueville may have gone out of fashion two generations back, for after all, he wrote about Anglo-American farmers of the 1830s, a different people from Americans today. But are we really so different in fundamental ways?

The evidence in Texas does not suggest that the people have altered all that much in 150 years.

Times change, fads and foibles change. Occupations and residences change. And issues over which Texans are prepared to fight change continually. But most of these changes in Texas have occurred less from evolution or choice than pressure. Virtually all the political and social reforms of the twentieth century enacted by government have been forced down the Anglo-Texan throat. Thus Texans have a different perspective of history and change from most Americans: They have been both conquerors and conquered on their own soil.

Texans have changed grudgingly on the whole, clinging to their own sense of being and worth. They have kept much of the Southern reverence for time and place, so lacking in today's rootless America. In a real sense, 1976 is 1876, or 1836 is 1776 in many Texan minds, and there is a feeling of rightness about this.

The social and intellectual turmoil of the 1960s, for example, made little stir among most Texans. Anti-Vietnam-War passions, anti-establishmentarianism, the civil rights and the feminist movements found scant nourishment in the social soil of Texas. Issues many Americans take seriously rarely get off campuses, and they do not dominate even there. The average Anglo-Texan has acceded to changes only when he could not do otherwise and has ignored them whenever he could do so successfully.

The frontier folk had a saying: "If it ain't broke don't fix it."

Most Texans, for all their articulate apostates and the criticism heaped upon them from the political and social Left, do not consider themselves or their culture – or the culture of their ancestors — broke. They infuriate others by putting a lot of old bourbon in new bottles, changing labels but sticking to the old recipes. And as the world continually changes and society oscillates between poles and extremes, Texans see themselves as both futuristic and traditional. They are often forced into hypocrisy, but this only makes them believe more strongly in their own rightness.

In the 1980s no Texas refugees are fleeing elsewhere, while hordes of Northerners and others are pouring in — so Texas must be doing something right.

It may be that during the coming years Texas attitudes on life, liberty, and the pursuit of happiness in business, government, and academe will have more impact on the nation than the nation will have on them.

Frontier-honed minds accept almost nothing based on hypothesis or theory. When things work, the Texas mind accepts them, even seizes them eagerly. It is important always to remember that the Texan mentality is intelligent, but utterly unintellectual. The oil lies under the ground, or it doesn't; the money is there or it ain't; talk is fine but changes nothing. Talk, including Texas brag, is really an art form or an entertainment. Serious business always involves action.

When someone brings forth a better mousetrap, Texans will buy it — and maybe the factory. But when other Americans suggest that the America of 1776 and 1836 was seriously flawed in its society and attitudes, Texans are not comfortable with such a thought, even though they may agree with it.

A greatly oversold idea has been the one that Texans, out of their movement from farm to town to metropolis, will belatedly follow the same social and economic courses as Americans in the older cities of the East. It has been suggested, hoped for, and demanded for years that Texan society grow into the national mainstream, with a greater belief in corporate community, a breakdown of puritan notions of self-reliance, a lessening of the sense of peoplehood that makes color and ethnic bars so impenetrable, and the rise of an urban upper-middle class with something of the same mindsets as those of Washington, D.C. or the suburbs surrounding Boston.

Very little, if any, of this seems to be happening in the Texas metropolitan maelstrom. Texans have certainly had to make enormous adjustments in the transition from purely rural life and values and the small-community relationships of the past. In the great city the Texan can be as much a face in the lonely crowd as any other American, and a person can get away with more in Houston than one can in Muleshoe or Liberty, sexually and socially, just as an Iowan can live a different life-style in Los Angeles. However, the visible social changes are not the result of urban life alone. Many of them are occurring also in the small towns, as a sort of general American social phenomenon; these include altered mores and the changing nature of the American nuclear family.

But few of these easily seen and often reported changes seem to reflect much change in world view, and in the largest urban areas where the Texan is emerging in a larger, dynamic society, he is making the cities peculiarly Texan — or more accurately, creating a dominant Southwestern pattern.

The Texan metropolis is not the nineteenth-century city, a city that industrialism and pre-auto transportation built. As that kind of city deteriorates — and as the older cores of Texas towns and cities everywhere suffer from the same sort of urban decay and demoralization, there is being created a new, different kind of urbanity.

The new city is a place in which its residents are not separated or isolated from the surrounding territory; in fact, the Texas and Southwestern cities simply rise up from or merge into the plains. This is a city that runs more to endless, sprawling suburbs, residential and commercial, than to tight or distinguishable neighborhoods. It has none of the feel of the older city — a thing that bewilders and bothers urbanites from other places. Paris may make Parisians, New York, New Yorkers, but Houston and Dallas continue to create Texans.

Texas is not replicating older patterns in urbanization, and Texans are not becoming soft-talking Yankees.

The pattern of urbanization is part of a new American process that has little in common with the older cities of the North or Midwest. This is just beginning to be seen, and it is beginning to be recognized that the problems of Texas cities are not the same as those of Cincinnati or Chicago. Texas has more to learn from Albuquerque, Phoenix, and San Diego, and they from it, than from Boston or Baltimore.

Texas cities belong to an emerging Sunbelt mainstream that now stretches from the Gulf of Mexico to the Pacific, reflecting a definite, different form of American society.

Almost all these cities really comprise two cities. This is not just a division between rich and poor, or directing and supporting classes. The first city, usually physically separated from the other and located in another part of town, contains an Anglo population that has adjusted to or can cope with the myriad complexities of modern organization and technology — essentially prosperous, remaining socially conservative, dominated by its traditional work ethic. This city creates green swards, glittering shopping malls, streams of auto-choked freeways, square miles of expensive new housing, clean, dispersed small plants and factories, and equally dispersed glass office buildings. Except among some newcomers from other regions, this city so far has developed little or nothing of the traditional, conventional urban upper-middle-class liberalism of Eastern cities — a fact that confounds some newspaper editors and other media executives who want to preserve both a local market and gain national intellectual respectability.

This city tends to believe in America as it is, not as it might or should be.

The other city within the city is more and more made up of basically unskilled workers, largely ethnic or racial minorities. The new Texas city creates an insatiable market for construction and service labor, filled in some cases preferably by undocumented or illegal aliens. The city creates vast numbers of jobs, but rarely the rewards for unskilled labor that, for example, assembly-line workers have won in industrial areas. The light industrial, high technology industries do not use assembly-line labor; and industrialists such as garment makers who operate in Texas cities usually do so precisely to take advantage of cheaper, non-unionized work forces.

In certain ways, the new Southwestern city resembles the burgeoning metropoli of some Third World countries – in fact, these social patterns have invaded the so-called First World almost everywhere.

The Anglo-Texan and hundreds of thousands of newcomers to the state seem to be fitting comfortably into this new-old society. However, while the cosmetic changes are noted daily and books and articles galore are published about Texas, most of the fundamental facts go almost unnoticed. They rarely appear in Texan or any other literature.

Old themes still dominate Texan observation and writing: the land, the rural society, the tall tale, the eternal frontier-life saga. There is very little about the current realities, the emergence of a *Texan* metropolitan culture and society, based on the old but developing differently from the cities of the past.

New careers, the adjustment and assimilation of newly arrived out-of-staters, the course of the Texan family, the place of religion and church in daily life, the uneasy confrontation with the new underclass and brown and black minorities – all these draw less attention in newspapers than an ephemeral "Texas chic" or a current retail sales or oil boom. They are not treated by serious writers at all, some of whom have, however, concentrated upon the problems of the past generation and the decay of the small Texas town.

This of course is not unusual. The great nineteenth-century novelists wrote of preceding, not their own, generations, and no doubt in time the currents moving present-day Texas will be treated from a future perspective, whether by Texans or others does not matter.

Meanwhile, Texas is growing explosively in the 1980s, a fact that will inevitably make certain kinds of changes. The Anglo-Texan culture, quite possibly, may be not so much changed as diluted — though cultures, once set, are very stubborn things.

Population growth is nothing new to Texas. Between 1850 and 1860 the state grew by 184 percent, and again between 1870 and 1880 the population almost doubled. This growth came in a formative, frontier period, of course, to a largely empty land, and since 90 percent of it derived from the same source, the South, it tended to be assimilative and socially reinforcing. The Alabamian refugees of 1870 fitted in easily with the Tennessean borderers of the 1830s. But while Texas grew steadily from both natural increase and continual in-migration after the vast frontier movements of the nineteenth century, native births were more important than immigration for about a century.

During the depression of the 1930s, growth was only about 10 percent, and after a brief spurt during and following the World War II years, it tapered off again. Until 1970 or even a few years afterward, in-migration was not really a significant factor in the growth of Texas cities.

This changed radically during the last years of the 1970s. The state population increased by more than three million, to a total of 14,228,383 in 1980. This marked a 27 percent increase for the decade against a national population increase of 11 percent; Texas acquired more new people than any other state except California. This was the largest numerical increase ever recorded, and the largest percentage increase in 70 years.

Buried in these figures is a startling fact. Between 1950 and 1970 more than 90 percent of all increase came from native births, but between 1970 and 1980, in-migration accounted for 58.3 percent, natural increase representing only 41.7 percent of the total growth of Texas' population.

An unprecedented number of non-Texans had suddenly appeared in the state, and the impact cannot yet be ascertained. Furthermore, in-migration has continued strongly. While projections are never entirely valid, the trend suggests a potential state population of 22 million by the year 2000 – a percentage growth of 55 percent, and most of it from sources outside the state.

In a highly urbanized society, this has created a population explosion, and the possibility that Texas may soon be as much affected by in-migrants as Florida or California, where newcomers have enormously changed native societal patterns.

The reasons for in-migration are many, but essentially simple. Some of it stems from the Sunbelt syndrome, the movement of Americans to warmer climes; but the major reason has been the favorable economic climate in Texas. And as more and more businesses move to, or are founded in Texas, this growth feeds upon itself; it creates its own dynamism. One boom in oil or real estate may fade, but another is usually not far distant on the horizon. Whatever happens to the national economy, Texas will probably add more new people between 1980 and 2000 than all the nine states together that makes up the Northeast.

The composition of this growth, however, is interesting and in many ways reassuring for Texans. The above figures do not reflect illegal aliens, mainly out of Mexico, estimates of which run from 500,000 to 3,000,000 – in any case, the figures are guesswork from various state agencies.

The great majority of people moving into Texas are Anglo, younger than the national average, and they possess higher than average technical skills and earn higher than average incomes. They come mainly from the traditional sources and places. Fifty-three percent of all migrants came from the South and West – ten percent from California, undoubtedly reflecting a large number of expatriate Texans returning home. Twenty-one percent arrived from the Midwest, and only eight percent from the Northeastern region.

Texas is not being overrun by Yankees, although it may seem so to some residents.

The newer in-migration is surprisingly much like the old, coming primarily from neighboring states, reflecting social and cultural patterns similar to the Texan. The new migrants are no longer seeking land as such, but certainly are looking for property and opportunity, and they are very susceptible to the scent of empire. A great many enter Texas to start new businesses, or to expand businesses established elsewhere. In a few places, notably Houston, many of the newcomers tend to be corporate employees, but this does not make up the general pattern.

Thus most of the newcomers reinforce rather than disrupt basic Texan attitudes and social relationships.

There are some economic refugees in this horde, of course, especially in the 1980s. There is already evidence that those coming from the industrial heartland are much less likely to succeed, fall in love with, or remain in Texas. Many were drawn by a sort of streets-paved-with-gold syndrome, a Texas mystique played up by newspapers and other media in the North during the deep recessions that have wracked industrial America. Most never understood the two-tiered nature of the Texas economy, or the ephemeral quality of the oil and construction booms of the 1970s, or the wage levels for unskilled labor. There have apparently been as many departures of unskilled workers from Texas recently as there have been arrivals, the number of those leaving having been accelerated by the lack of public welfare and social services.

Many Americans do not understand the true nature of an economic frontier which traditionally rewards capital and enterprise but not necessarily labor. While unemployment remained low in Texas in the 1970s and even in 1982 was well below the national average, the types and pay of most Texas jobs have not endeared the state to displaced union members from Pittsburg or Detroit.

The sheer number of newcomers, however, has been destabilizing in many parts of Texas. This has had definite political effects. Too many people have strained the free market and the *laissez-faire* philosophy of local government. The rapid growth of cities has caused congestion, housing problems, pressure on all social services and utilities. It has threatened the relaxed life-styles still current even in the large cities, and especially the relaxed practices of Texan urban management.

Courts, jails, schools, streets, drainage, prisons, and pollution controls have become inadequate across much of Texas; localities simply cannot cope with the new numbers. Some communities experienced temporary problems with excesses of job-seekers, first the oil-patch towns in West Texas, later the huge cities such as Houston. They have become burdened with transients and indigents, with proliferating crime and misery. Even in places where the influx is permanent and essentially healthy economically, it has still strained the old reluctance of Texans to tax themselves for public services.

The rise of a new homosexual community in Houston, where the money is, has drawn more attention — but the floods caused by a paving-over explosion of raw land with inadequate provisions from drainage, the hazard of foul air, and the sheer inability to drive to work over clogged freeways bothers the citizenry in far worse ways.

Here the election of Kathy Whitmire, a woman mayor, fiscally conservative but pledged to end the old do-nothing policies of previous administrations, showed a clear impatience with ways that no longer seem to work.

Whitmire's sex and her heralded support from "alternative life style" communities may have obscured the fact that the basic issue in this city had become the development of policy intervention by civic government — something new to a city without even zoning laws. Women have often played prominent roles in Texas politics and Texas business, from governor to mayors to the heads of large enterprises and foundations in this male-value-dominated society. However, such women almost invariably themselves hold or at least project male values — they are not at odds with the old frontier where women always played an essential part.

Houston and the other new cities may be economically and socially conservative, their citizens clinging to economic liberty and low taxes, but the complexities of modern urban sprawl require adjustments, including planning. Political pressure is intensified by newcomers who arrive accustomed to expensive civic services and demand improvements.

The physical problems such as housing, energy, streets, sewers, drainage, and water are all solvable, though water in the long run may be limiting to growth. Water supply is critical in most parts of Texas. The state has always left this up to individual communities; cities and towns acquire and develop their own supply without state assistance, but this too may have to change.

Crowding in the largest cities has already begun to produce spin-offs. Large corporations have begun to bypass Houston, searching out smaller urban areas for offices and headquarters, while polls shows that a majority of all Texans, despite the outrage of real estate and development interests and boosters in general, by 1981 were less euphoric over new growth than worried about its impact on the traditional Texan way of life. Texan attitudes are rapidly shaping up along the lines of those of Western states such as Colorado, at least so far as continued population growth is concerned.

The creation of the Texas 2000 Commission in 1980 marked the first entry of the state into anything resembling resource and economic planning. Concerned with explosive growth and a lack of data, Governor Clements empowered the Commission to identify and project changes in Texas' population, natural resources, economy and service infrastructure over the next twenty years; to develop and analyze alternative state policy response; and to propose solutions to long-range problems.

The Texas 2000 Commission began its work by addressing the problems of water — seen as most critical statewide — energy, agriculture, transportation, research and development, government finance, and relations with Mexico. In the vagaries of state politics its report, issued in 1982, may or may not be acted upon. However, Texas has taken at least a first step toward rational planning for the future.

What sort of cities and state will emerge by the year 2000, of course, is still a question. As with long-range weather forecasting, there are too many variables.

Meanwhile, the old provincial culture, mores, and moral values are coming under perhaps more strain than physical resources, or Texas politics and business. The puritan tradition that makes Texans uncomfortable with high culture or even feel guilty about demanding fine cuisine (Texan cities are filled with high-priced, pretentious restaurants offering fare that would be sneered at in San Francisco or Montreal) may fade under affluence and a growing awareness and taste for better things. The frontier concepts of what is manly and what is not tend to weaken when Texas money comes to be increasingly inherited rather than earned the hard way.

But even if Texans go the way of the Romans, they will go in ways peculiar to their time and place, Texas and the Southwest. Houston may look like other cities — Brooks Brothers suits and Midwestern accents on every corner — but it will not become a new New York, nor will Dallas become a second Chicago. San Antonio in some sense will always remain a bigger Cotulla. Out of the blend of history, nativism, and newcomer will come a society with strong continuity to the past and to the Texas present, and it will be distinctly Texan.

The mystique of Texas is too strong. Texans could never implement their option to divide into five states because of this mystique which transcends mere local interests and political ambitions — and just as the Texans have remained a single, consciously unitary people for all their diversity, Texas will always remain Texas.

Sam Houston described Negro slavery as a curse from which America might never escape — and Texas, no more than the rest of America, has certainly not thrown off the incubus in the second century of black emancipation.

The first Texas colonists brought back slaves to perform essential labor they could not or would not do themselves. On an open frontier with open lands, white workers were almost unattainable and servile labor seemed as much the answer as it had to the Spaniards of the sixteenth century and the Virginians at Jamestown. Whatever slavery's course and future in the older South in the mid-nineteenth century, it was flourishing and economically profitable in Texas up to the Civil War, and it was only abolished by federal proclamation upon the arrival of a Union army of occupation in June, 1865.

Under the slave laws, black servants were basically chattels rather than persons forced to do involuntary labor. The arguments and views regarding the institution are regularly revived and revised, but slavery in Texas was not patriarchal with bonds of obligation between both master and servant. It was a system of the entrepreneurial exploitation of labor for profit, based on a law and society that was explicitly racist, in that the servitude of black people was justified by their racial inequality with whites.

Thus, the dichotomy existed of a genuine male, Caucasian democracy side by side with a slave society in which blacks had few more rights than mules.

While few Texas families owned slaves, they made up about 20 percent of the population, and the institution had a pervasive influence upon society and politics. Somewhat different attitudes toward slavery and slaves grew up between the Texas frontier and western counties and the Old-South extension to the east. The slave regions were accustomed to blacks and in those areas the main concern of whites was to keep the Negro population under control. The non-slave areas disliked both slaves and slavery and wanted to have nothing to do with either. These attitudes toward black Texans have persisted from 1865 to the present.

Bluntly put, the problem of Texas (and most of America) was what to do with the black population after it was freed. A majority of Texas whites considered the black no more equal than before. His labor was needed – and in many cases feared in free competition – but the color bar, centuries strong and buttressed by all the fears, hatreds, and dehumanizations of slavery, prevented any easy acceptance of the Negro into society.

None was made, or even seriously attempted, once military occupation ended in the North's having grown weary with Reconstruction.

The share-cropping solution "solved" the problem for many years. The former slaves now worked the land, often the same land, as free men, but in some ways as semi-serfs, bound both by debts and the lack of any other opportunity. Some blacks became cowhands; some established new, free-holding if impoverished communities near the towns (where their heirs sometimes later came into big money due to the appreciation of property values); most stayed on the old plantations under new masters and new arrangements.

The history of black-white relations from 1865 is complex, and does not always follow popular mythology. In the earlier years of emancipation – once former slaveowners were forced to accept the demise of the institution – there seems to have been little trouble and not much ill will. While the manipulation of the black vote by carpetbaggers during Reconstruction was the basis of Republican rule when most ex-Confederates were barred from the polls, no institutional bars were placed on black voting in the years that followed.

The agricultural crisis that began soon after exacerbated latent black-white antipathies as it did so much else. As more and more white farmers were themselves forced into tenantry, the color bar – the assumed superiority of the white man

— became increasingly more important to poor whites. This was not, at least in Texas, fostered by racist politicians at first. Rather, Populist leaders tried strenuously to weld both black and white voters into a significant power bloc in the poor man's interest. This totally failed due to white recalcitrance — and the effort certainly played a large part in what followed in Texas and in other Southern states, for the effort produced a lasting fear of black political power among both rich and poor. It was not until around the turn of the century, in the debacle of Populism, that all the institutional devices to separate the races and keep the blacks in a second-class status — the poll tax, the segregation laws, the "grandfather" clauses — were fully put in place.

Caste replaced servitude, in a logical if not defensible pattern of domination and discrimination.

The bulk of the black population remained on the farm until the early decades of the twentieth century. In the 1930s, during the Depression, share-cropping became more and more economically unfeasible for landowners; the trend was to consolidate small plots into larger blocks operated by relatively affluent white tenants able to exploit machinery. This period saw the wholesale movement of Texas blacks from the countryside into the smaller towns at first, and later, into the large cities and toward the North.

The first four decades of this century also reveal a generally dreadful treatment of Texas blacks during this displacement. The Negro shantytowns became places of persistent, internal violence, which white authorities ignored so long as it did not affect whites. When it did, retaliation was swift, brutal, and sometimes indiscriminate. Racial turmoil was common, and during those years Texas exceeded the Deep South in the number of recorded lynchings, the extralegal execution of suspected blacks, in which authorities either acquiesced or sometimes took part.

Peculiarly, this violence was more marked in Texas — on one occasion, a mob burned down a new jail in order to destroy a black suspect — because the Negro population was declining, in comparison to the white, and at the ratio of about ten to one it contained the perfect mix for violence. Mississippi and Alabama, meanwhile, did their own dreadful things with more discipline and decorum; only Georgia could compete with East Texas.

The violent phase ended by the 1940s. In some respects, it simply played itself out. The poverty and tensions of the 1930s eased; blacks moved from smaller communities into cities; dominant Anglo-Texan opinion grew ashamed of brutality, if not quite as ashamed of continued racial discrimination.

This bitter experience probably played its part when the legal color bars were banned by federal action in the 1950s and 1960s. Texans in high office and positions of power may not have lost their distaste for black equality, but they detested disorder and mob actions more. Texas saw almost none of the resistance to desegregation that flared in Arkansas or Alabama and other states, and while futile debates about interposition and states rights dragged on in the legislature, no officeholders abetted or encouraged defiance.

Also, while two-thirds of the population still lived east of the Colorado River, Texas was not entirely a "Southern" state. In some places the color bars were let down quietly before the laws were changed. In San Antonio and most southern and western counties where blacks were few and the establishment of a separate school system had proved costly and ridiculous, desegregation was regarded with relief.

The relative calm in Texas black ghettos through the national racial turmoil of the 1960s also showed that things had changed. No major Texas city had an explosion, for at least two reasons. One, local authorities were ready to put it down immediately, without temporizing, which was well understood by most local black leadership. Second, there *was* a black leadership in most Texas Negro communities — ironically, the color bar had fostered the development of a black middle class which had never been siphoned off into white society.

This black leadership — perhaps best illustrated by the career of Barbara Jordan in the state senate — tended to be pragmatic, essentially patriotic, much more inclined to work within the political establishment where many of its members won sincere respect, than to become lost in impossible dreams or Third World rhetoric. Yet it was too successful in its limited goals, too powerful, to be branded as a congregation of Uncle Toms.

By the 1980s black-white relations in Texas had reached a sort of stasis. Black political power was established in certain areas, even with a declining black population (in 1980 only 12 percent). This was accomplished with good humor; dominant opinion saw it as no threat. The black revolution of the 1960s did away with the old, emasculating humiliations, the back-of-the bus seating, the "nigger heaven" in the movie houses, the barring of blacks from respectable, middle-class employment. Blacks in Texas have shared, if not proportionately, in the general rise in prosperity. Houston has its black millionaires, however unlike the Texas stereotype they may be.

This does not mean that Texan society is anywhere close to honest integration or moving toward it. The societies are separate; only in politics and around a few universities is there anything approaching social admixture. Few whites of any class feel really comfortable in close proximity; and middle-class blacks, when truth is told, do not easily relax when admitted into white society. And yet, for every Texan who still in his heart thinks slavery was the best solution, perhaps a dozen believe that the blacks must, and should be, given a fair chance.

Here Texas indeed has changed and moved closer to the national, or at least Southwestern norm. The problem is not, most Texans think, to find love but rather to continue to work out a humanizing *modus vivendi.*

The other significant minority in Texas, the Hispanics or Mexican-Americans, presents quite a different aspect. Black problems and Hispanic problems, while both have been exacerbated by discrimination and poverty and are often lumped together, are not the same. And if black Texans are not a force for fundamental change in the whole society, the Mexican population, rapidly growing due to heavy, continued immigration and a higher birthrate and now reaching 21 percent of the state's population, shows an entirely different possibility.

Anglo-Texans have not yet confronted the "Mexican question" and the Mexican minority – but then, the majority of that minority has not yet really confronted Anglo-Texas.

Here the socio-economic problem is not racial or based on color differentiation, but cultural, which makes it at once more amenable but vastly more complex and slippery.

Despite myth and much Northern misunderstanding, the large Mexican presence in Texas (and in the Southwest) is recent. Only a few thousand people were transferred from Mexico to the United States in 1848, and throughout the nineteenth century this hardly increased. As late as 1900, less than five percent of the Texas population was of Mexican origin, and even along the border, Anglo-Americans were at least as numerous as the Spanish-speaking.

This changed, beginning with the massive development of the Lower Rio Grande Valley, with extensive agriculture and the processing of agricultural products. This coincided with overpopulation, hideous agrarian poverty, peasant oppression and finally, revolution in Mexico. The Southwest needed cheap labor to make it competitive with other regions nearer to markets, and it recruited this labor from below the Rio Grande.

In each year after 1900, more Mexicans came to Texas to work than had entered it throughout all the long centuries when the state was part of the Spanish world. Between 1900 and 1910 the Mexican population of Texas increased by 76 percent. During the next decade, 264,503 arrived, and more than 165,000 from 1920 to 1930 — officially. Most of the immigration, then as now, was entirely informal, but then there was no bar whatever on immigration from the Western Hemisphere into the United States. Few of the first generation ever became citizens — but they stayed.

This people, hardy, gregarious, polite, accustomed to suffering, living and emigrating in extended family groups, predominately of the *pelado* ("skinned") or peasant class, was fiercely exploited by American, but not by Mexican, standards. In Texas at fifty cents per day, a family might make more money than it could ever hope to earn on the Mexican plateau — a pattern that has continued throughout the century, with proportional inflation.

The Texans who imported them, much like the Yankees who imported Italians or Chinese to work on railroads, never thought beyond the immediate need for labor. To a great extent, the Anglos tended to equate Mexican workers with Negroes — useful, provided they did not meddle in the white folks' business.

In the 1920s a University of Texas study reported that Mexicans were migrating *en masse*, and that, unlike Italians or Germans, they were not assimilating. Their schooling was not encouraged, but they also had no tradition of education. Above all, Mexican immigrants clung to the Spanish language, which created an immense barrier to any sort of cultural assimilation.

Nobody in Anglo-Texas paid much attention to the potential problem until the 1960s, when ethnicity became fashionable nationally — and by this time the Mexican presence in Texas had become too massive to be ignored.

In many ways, the path and progress of Mexican immigrants in Texas has been similar to that of blacks. Both peoples were brought in to perform agricultural labor. Until the 1930s, most Mexican-Americans lived in the rural areas, and the same forces that displaced the blacks took them on the long trek from country to town to metropolitan area, and to ghetto-like *barrios* in the core cities. Mexican immigrants, their children and grandchildren, met much of the same social, economic, and educational discrimination — until 1949, many Texas communities officially put "Mexicans" in separate school classes, if not separate school systems.

However, there was never an absolute color bar as with Negroes. Mexican-Americans come of varying racial ancestry, ranging from pure European to pure American Indian, and when such things counted they were listed as "White" under Texan law. There were never official bars to intermarriage, although for a long time, except in the highest or lowest classes, this remained socially unthinkable. And many, if not most, of the nineteenth-century Hispanics in Texas became well assimilated. Some were rich and never suffered any form of discrimination, although the long-settled members of the serving classes got lumped in with the hordes of new agrarian laborers.

In the sea change that has affected racial and ethnic attitudes and practices in Texas since the 1960s, and as Mexican-American political power has increased dramatically (it controls most of south Texas, and in disputed state-wide races Democrats simply must carry the Mexican-American vote to win against the Republican cities) color bars and overt discrimination have almost vanished. This does not mean a Mexican-American will be taken into an old-line club any more than a black or newly-arrived Yankee who has not married into a Texan family, but it does mean that the problem facing the Hispanic minority in Texas is much less color than a classic cultural confrontation.

The Mexican minority in Texas, and across the Southwest, shows marked resemblances to the French population in Canada, centered in the province of Quebec. In Quebec, 80 percent of the people are French-speaking, but 80 percent of the property and business enterprise are controlled by Anglo-Canadians. The *Québécois* have held all political offices for generations, but peasant-derived, with a different ethos from the Anglos, they have remained a blue-collar and peasant mass sprinkled with a few intellectuals, all enormously discontented with their situation.

The Mexican-American came into a land where most of the property and all the systems were Anglo-Saxon; he became a majority in South Texas and makes up 45 percent of the San Antonio metropolitan area; he can elect mayors and sheriffs and dog catchers — but unless and until he can speak English with a native accent and cope with an Anglo economy he remains something of a stranger in his own country.

Texas' Mexican-Americans are no longer denied assimilation; the fact is that many, possibly a majority, reject it, in the demand that they can continue to be Mexican in culture, and the hope that they can remain Spanish-speaking without paying penalties. This is a serious form of cleavage, because there is a vast and historic gulf between the Mexican and Anglo cultures.

Hispanics see the Anglo-Saxon (though this view does not, oddly, apply to Anglo women) as cold, dry, graceless, unmanly, and relentlessly scheming, remorselessly active. To the Anglo-Texan the Mexican seems feckless, utterly lacking in entrepreneurial and self-starting ability, given to rhetoric, undisciplined and prone to make a mess of things — just as Mexicans have done with the nation of Mexico.

The Anglo ethic is simple, and Anglos who do not actually follow it still ascribe to it religiously: *Work is a virtue beyond any necessity; getting ahead is a must; competition is healthy; wealth is a reasonable, if not the only reasonable basis for status.*

Mexicans of all classes find themselves uneasy with such a stark world view, which seems to leave out certain essentials.

In any event, the Mexican-American has found it hard to compete with, if not comprehend, the graceless Anglo-Saxon.

The tendency in Texas towns and cities is for there to be two communities, each pillared, each formed of numerous classes, with easy social mixture only at the very top, with a long-settled Mexican-American upper class that in some cases may be reasonably *agringado* or *inglesado*, that is to say, Anglicized.

Anglos and Mexican-Texans work together easily, the Anglo usually but not always in charge, but they drink together less comfortably. And when the Mexican-American does not speak the native tongue, they never associate, because Anglo women seldom learn more Spanish than to direct servants, while the Anglo-Texan's often fluent grasp of Tex-Mex rarely extends beyond the needs of the ranch or workshop.

And this Texan is no more going to learn Spanish, in the long run, than the *Québécois* is going to give up his native tongue for English, or the Flemish-speaking Belgian adopt French.

Because of the relative newness of the Hispanic in-migration, the newness of the Texan acceptance of Mexicans (if they try to assimilate), and the continuing effect of massive immigration (in which some long-settled families intermarry with recent arrivals or even illegal entrants and fourth-generation children continue to learn Spanish as their first language) it is impossible to project the course of this cultural relationship.

In South Texas, especially, a new Quebec may be in the making, or perhaps a new Alsace. On the other hand, there is strong evidence that in many of the smaller towns and cities the children of Mexican-Americans do learn English without the stigma of *barrio* accents – television is a wonderful cultural leveler – and that the American ethic may not be far behind. Culture, after all, stems primarily from language, and world views are largely formed by the concepts of the mother tongue.

Politically, the emergence of Mexican-American officialdom has not made all that much of a change. There has been no "brown wave" or "red dawn," despite the over-publicized and abortive political capture of the small south

Texas town of Crystal City by *Raza Unida*, an overtly racist Mexican political movement comprised primarily of academics and laborers. Hispanic politicians, like most black leadership, are wary of "Kill the gringo" rhetoric. The Democratic Party co-opts the majority, thus providing a great stabilizing factor, while some seek quicker promotion if less opportunity with the Republicans.

The rural counties that have come under Mexican-Texan political sway seem to be managed just about as well — or badly — as those still run by Anglos — and anyone who thinks that all Texas Hispanics are alike or that they form a monolithic movement must be ignorant of politics in the Hispanic world.

In some cases, the emergence of Hispanic political leaders, such as Henry Cisneros, the first modern mayor of San Antonio of Mexican ancestry, is both healthy and helpful. Such men and women ease ancient Mexican-American feelings of humiliation; ambitious and energetic, they are thoroughly integrated into the system and understand its realities and possibilities. Cisneros is not quite a "Texan," certainly not of the old school — but he is in no sense a "Mexican," either. He appears to be a man who is alive to the thrust of the new Southwestern metropolis, its beauties, strengths, and failings, and his outlook and ethos are those of the new Texan metropolitan who understands both the *barrio* and the prosperous suburban sprawlings.

The Hispanic minority, already a majority in many places, will probably not bring as much change to Texas as some fear, and others hope. It will throw off domination by Anglos — but it is not likely to dominate Anglos, for after all, this is still Anglo country. Assimilation in a real sense — although hated by some Mexican-American intellectuals and politicians, will probably continue to be spurred by economic opportunity, for it is not lost on some Texas Mexicans that the Cubans in Miami, by becoming Americanized, have made more economic progress in one generation than has *la raza* in an entire century. And that young men and women who speak educated native Texan, or even American, more easily find employers eager to open for them the doors to opportunity.

Fusion is possible — as with Saxons and Normans — but it is not likely. There is no Hispanic educational, financial, or scientific establishment in the United States, nor likely to be no matter how many Hispanics arrive. The successful Mexican-American must make his way in an Anglo world; therefore, the thrust is all toward effective assimilation.

The Mexican-American may create a lasting subculture within the Texan culture, as the Texan has made his own subculture within the American — but they will both be part of the whole.

For some masses of Hispanics, as well as blacks trapped in the core cities, there seems to be no escape or perfect solution in this generation. The new city draws and holds thousands of people who are ill-equipped to succeed in this — or any other — modern milieu. This will continue to be a festering American, as well as Texan, problem.

Americans, however, tend to be very much a present-minded and problem-oriented people. Under the pressure of present problems, they find it easy to lose perspective. The perspective that is sometimes lost, in Texas, is the one that brings into full view the tremendous improvements wrought by change since the 1940s and 1950s.

Whatever the problems and antagonisms of today, they are much less than the crudities and hatreds of the past. There is a growing understanding among all races that many kinds of people have come to Texas, and all have come to stay. The sour moods of the impoverished agrarian frontier have vastly improved in the prosperity of the new economic frontier. The dominant mood in Texas is not to hold anyone down, but to let no such nonsense get in the way of business.

Prosperity can be a greater leveler than poverty, and this is what Texans of all classes, colors, and creeds trust will come to pass.

CONCLUSION

These, then, are seven major keys to understanding Texas. There are others — a true list could be infinite — but if one understands something of the people, the frontier, the land, the economy, the society, the politics, and the ways of change in a country, one may understand it even better than the native, and without even visiting it.

Americans often have trouble understanding Texas because they refuse to look on the state in the light of its own history and prejudices, preferring to impose their own instead.

We need to see a people, like all peoples in many ways brave and admirable, in others mean, narrow, and limited, who entered a harsh and dangerous country, fighting desperate, essentially cultural battles when their numbers were still small, who asserted their independence from one civilization while keeping another race in bondage, who conquered all, and who then, over a century both from war and from forces they could not — and still cannot — control, saw their pride humbled. We need to see a people made into a people, to understand why they cling to that sense of peoplehood — a race, conquerors and conquered, never entirely surrendering their soil, with an almost sacred sense of that soil.

We must see the nature of the colonial Texas economy, the continuing, ancient bias against social organization. We must recognize a population that still remembers where its grandparents are buried, and that changed only superficially in a cultural sense as it moved from land to town, from horse to automobile.

Then, perhaps, many things fall into place: the pride, the politics, the prejudice, the patriotism — for land and people and symbolic nation, although never for regimes or ideologies — the essential conservatism underlying even occasionally radical politics, the deep if unarticulated sense of territoriality, of peoplehood, the eternal feeling for time and place, and above all, for place and people without regard to time.